Alison Tedford

T0268040

STAY WOKE, NOT BROKE

Protect Your Brand in Today's Business Climate

Self-Counsel Press
(a division of)
International Self-Counsel Press Ltd.
Canada USA

Self-Counsel Press acknowledges the financial support of the Government of Canada through the Canada Book Fund (CBF) for our publishing activities.

We also gratefully recognize the Coast Salish, Tsleil-Waututh, Squamish, Sto:lo, Musqueam, and Nooksack peoples, on whose land our offices are located.

Printed in Canada.

First edition: 2022

Library and Archives Canada Cataloguing in Publication

Title: Stay woke, not broke : protect your brand in today's business climate / Alison Tedford.

Names: Tedford, Alison, author.

Series: Self-Counsel business series.

Description: First edition. | Series statement: Self-Counsel business series

Identifiers: Canadiana (print) 20210381914 | Canadiana (ebook) 20210381981 | ISBN 9781770403390 (softcover) | ISBN 9781770405301 (EPUB) | ISBN 9781770405318 (Kindle)

Subjects: LCSH: Social responsibility of business. | LCSH: Business ethics. | LCSH: Diversity in the workplace. | LCSH: Cancel culture.

Classification: LCC HD60 .T43 2022 | DDC 658.4/08—dc23

Self-Counsel Press
(a division of)
International Self-Counsel Press Ltd.

North Vancouver, BC	Bellingham, WA
Canada	USA

CONTENTS

NOTICE TO READERS

Laws are constantly changing. Every effort is made to keep this publication as current as possible. However, the author, the publisher, and the vendor of this book make no representations or warranties regarding the outcome or the use to which the information in this book is put and are not assuming any liability for any claims, losses, or damages arising out of the use of this book. The reader should not rely on the author or the publisher of this book for any professional advice. Please be sure that you have the most recent edition.

ACKNOWLEDGMENTS AND DEDICATION

I am grateful for Kelly Diels, Sonya Perkins, the OneLAX Team, and Megan Hale for their time, expertise, and role modeling. I would like to acknowledge my business coach Hillary Weiss Presswood for guiding me; and for Dusti Arab, Briar Harvey, Alison Shaughnessy Warlitner, and Rachel Barbic who helped me through my first program launch.

Most of all, I would like to thank my clients past, present, and future for their brave commitment to a better world.

This book is dedicated to the memory of Smoky-Top (Willie Seaweed), my great-great grandfather, the guiding light from my past, and to my son Liam Tedford, the guiding light of my future.

PREFACE

People were protesting. And for good reason. Another Black man — this time it was George Floyd — had been killed by police. The footage was shocking. The anger and pain were palpable. Rage was warranted. From social media news feeds to city streets, cries for justice reverberated.

This had been going on for far too long and people all over were hurting. In social media posts they shared what was in their hearts. They talked about it in Facebook groups, tweeted about it on Twitter, and poured their hearts out on Instagram. The business community took notice.

Responses from allies started to pop up. A black square was posted on social media feeds everywhere to mark the moment, followed by a period of silence to not interrupt the important conversations taking place. We were all supposed to be "listening and learning." But it wasn't enough. Those words were hollow without action.

In some cases, the action taken made things worse. Online business icons saw their communities turn on them as they tried to enforce "no politics" zones in their social media spaces. This didn't sit well and felt like silencing. In an attempt to right the ship, many leaders posted apologies with promises to do better.

In some cases, these apologies felt as hollow as the black square posts. Marked by tears, these influencers expressed their regret over the way they handled the situation, sometimes sparking even more rage.

Attempts to be "business as usual" under these circumstances were not looked upon favorably. People needed space to process what happened. They needed to express their grief and explain how the tragedy impacted their ability to be productive, to feel safe, and to know that the people whose programs they invested in cared about what could happen to them.

Attempts to contain the outrage were ineffective. People only got more mad. They left groups; hit unfollow; and stopped investing their time, money, and attention in those they felt weren't supportive, empathetic, or understanding enough in that moment of grief.

Digital empires crumbled. There were some people who complained about "cancel culture," like the expectations that online gurus were faced with were unreasonable. How were they to know that they could no longer be silent about something that seemingly had nothing to do with the business they were in?

The bar had been raised. It was no longer acceptable to be silent. The impulse to be neutral or to stop uncomfortable conversations to maintain "good vibes only" wasn't going to cut it anymore. The world had changed and doing business had to change too.

Other business owners watched this failure to respond adequately and they got nervous. They didn't want to get canceled, or for their audience to be upset. They didn't want to lose money or the valuable audience they had already invested in building.

At the same time, they didn't know what to do. They could see that mistakes had been made but they weren't sure exactly what they were or how to avoid them and they didn't know how to respond in a way that wasn't going to be seen as performative. They were so afraid to make a mistake and they didn't know how to lead in this situation.

I watched the confusion unfold and in my small business, decided to release an offering that helped other business owners learn how to navigate the standards they were going to be held to. I called it the "Summer of social justice series: Stay Woke, Not Broke." It was a 21-day program and it discussed how to make a diversity statement, how to plan for social justice conversations, and how to moderate inclusive communities. The program included lectures, room to ask questions, and a community of business owners with good intentions who needed more support to do the right thing.

The program sold out and though it was very well-received, I found that it was too fast for people to implement without one-on-one support. The timing: A slower summertime pace plus the reality of running a business during COVID-19 meant that people weren't able to implement at the speed they hoped.

As things were implemented, more questions came up and, in order to support business owners to be truly successful, I needed to extend the length of the program and provide opportunities for one-to-one strategy sessions that were specific to their business so that they could get the full value of my support.

Almost a year later, the program was reoffered as "More Than Words Inclusion," with the addition of three strategy sessions and done-for-you copy so that people could have a professional diversity statement. Many business owners had already adopted a small business pledge by entrepreneur Rachel Rodgers, which was very good but not as specific to their business.

They hadn't taken the time to reflect on how those commitments applied to their businesses and how they talked about it. They didn't know how to talk about what they did through an intersectional lens. They didn't know how to "do better" as they observed audience demand. They needed more help.

Stay Woke, Not Broke was created as a response to questions such as, "How do I sell during these uncertain times without looking like a jerk?," "How do I talk about my values without looking like a bandwagon jumper?," and "How do I take meaningful action towards inclusion in my business?."

For small-business owners who don't have the luxury of being able to afford a full-time diversity person, these expectations can feel overwhelming. Not having equivalent resources to a large organization can feel like a barrier to doing anything. Paralysis by analysis leaves people feeling stuck.

The program offerings I developed became the basis of this book. My goal with the program and its book is to help business owners make better choices, become leaders of inclusion, and learn to navigate the enhanced accountabilities that are expected of business owners now and in the future.

Business as usual isn't good enough and business owners can no longer afford to be neutral. It isn't even enough to be a business owner with an opinion on social justice, there's an expectation of actual meaningful action.

A Family Legacy of Justice: My Personal Connection

I am a Kwakiutl woman, and in my culture, copper is a symbol of both wealth and justice. It was prized for its value and people would break it in ceremony when something needed a remedy. Money and justice were inextricably tied in my traditions through this symbolism and it is my belief that is not an accident and deeply important.

My great-great-grandfather had a nickname, which was Smoky-Top, because when people were doing things that were not consistent with protocol during ceremony, he would stand in front of the fire in the big house and tell people what they should be doing. It looked like smoke was coming from the top of his head as he stood there teaching people.

His traditional name translates to "Right Maker." He was a hereditary chief and a leader. He taught people how to uphold what culture required. He was also a humorist who knew how to make people laugh. The more I learn about him, the more I think we would have gotten along.

It was in the spirit of his desire to make things right and teach people the way that I undertook this work. I wanted to be a "right maker," too. My great-great-grandfather was also known as a distributor of wealth and I wanted to be known as the same. I wanted to be somebody who helped people make money while doing the right thing.

Another piece of my great-great-grandfather's experience was that he made money by creating masks for potlatch ceremonies. What is most striking about this is that at the time potlatch ceremonies were actually illegal and so was owning masks. The potlatch ban ran from 1885 to 1951.

My great-great-grandfather's entire artistic legacy as far as masks went was mostly illegal. But doing the right thing while making money was a value that he held. He did it anyway and he didn't concern himself with White men's laws. He charged modest prices for his artistic commissions. He also sold his art to museums, and you can still find his work in museums all around the world and in private collections of serious art collectors.

He was incredibly subversive in that he didn't concern himself with the legalities of what he did because he felt a stronger imperative to uphold culture and do the right thing even if it wasn't the legal thing.

Northwest Coast artist Andy Everson shared a story of Christmas potlatch arrests in a Facebook post to contextualize what was happening at the time. It referred to a letter between government offices from 1921 that spoke of how First Nations people should be dissuaded from "dancing." The reference of dancing was to the potlatch ceremony, which was so much more than just a dance.

"Our entire society revolved around the Potlatch. Simply put, our people publicly displayed our ceremonial prerogatives — including songs, dances, names and positions — in front of an assembled group of invited guests. In return for publicly validating those prerogatives, the guests were paid as witnesses. This had the effect of redistributing wealth throughout the communities. This wasn't just about dancing — his was our entire socio-economic system. The Canadian government in their attempts at genocide and assimilation sought to destroy our way of life.

"One hundred years ago, this letter was written. Ten days later, Chief Dan Cranmer hosted one of the largest potlatches ever held on the coast. The Indian Agent directed the RCMP to arrest many of the people involved in that potlatch—motivated by this letter and others like it and emboldened by the Canadian anti-potlatch law. In the end, 22 of our chiefs, knowledge keepers and noble women were sent to serve sentences at Oakalla Prison. Over 600 priceless masks and ceremonial pieces were confiscated from our people and sent away to Ottawa."

One Christmas morning, all sorts of people were arrested for holding a potlatch which was a gift-giving ceremony in its most simplistic explanation. They were asked to hand over their masks and regalia.

What struck me most about the Christmas Day arrests was that exchanging gifts is a tradition in Christian and mainstream households but doing so while Indigenous and in the context of potlatch was illegal.

This experience really illustrated that the right thing and the legal thing were not always synonymous and that people needed strong leadership to show them the way. My great-great-grandfather's approach was shaped by the temper that he was known for but he was also a storyteller and generous with his gifts.

A book called *Smoky-Top: The Art and Times of Willie Seaweed* by Bill Holm (Douglas & MacIntyre, 1983), examines his artistic and cultural legacy and was the way through which I got to know a man who died long before I was born. Willie Seaweed was my great-great-grandfather, Joe his son, and Henry his grandson. Henry is my grandfather and a cultural leader in his own right.

I see the work that I do in the business world as being a continuation of the legacy of my family. I may not be standing in front of a fire as I explain what to do, and I try to approach the work that I do with a strong "mom" energy that encourages people that they can do hard things. The spirit is the same. I want to help people do better.

I also feel deeply connected to my great-great-grandfather's artistic style, which was developed in part due to the geographic isolation of his community. He lived in a community called Blunden Harbour which was difficult to access by boat and that meant that artists in his area developed a certain style which flourished without the influence of others. I could relate to this because at the time of this writing there is a global pandemic that is causing deep isolation and it is in this isolation that my work is being crafted.

Through the magic of the internet, I am still connected to others but the isolation of this time has brought so many moments of deep contemplation and the ability to develop theory mostly uninterrupted by social demands.

My great-great grandfather's work was described as flamboyant and innovative. These weren't just masks that were carved that were immobile, they contained pulley systems and actually moved in unexpected ways. I hope to bring a similar spirit of innovation and flamboyance to this work.

Smoky-Top didn't sign his work, it was recognizable due to his technique. He was an artist who used precision instruments to produce beautiful art. He measured things using compass points and you can tell something was made by him (generally) by the presence of three compass points in the eye of the mask; he took great care to be consistent in his approach.

He autographed his work with his excellence. I aspire to that level of quality in my consulting work. My compass points are the framework that I apply in my work to provide consistent outcomes for people looking to elevate their understanding of social justice and business. I may not be considered a cultural leader in my family's traditions but I do hope to be one in business.

My Experience Integrating Social Justice into Government and Business

I got my first government job when I was 18 and I ended up working in the federal public service for over a decade. I did a lot of work on Indigenous issues, from working on residential school issues to working on projects to bring more Indigenous culture into the prison system.

My role involved taking the bureaucratic and translating it for cultural people, and taking culture and helping bureaucrats understand it. It was like translation essentially, trying to help people understand each other and trying to figure out how policy and cultural objectives could be achieved within a bureaucratic framework.

From supporting spiritual service delivery that goes beyond a pan-Indigenous approach, to looking at how policy could be culturally sensitive and examining corporate objectives and matching them to daily activities to identify the ways that inclusion goals could be reached incrementally, my work was about infusing culture into an institution.

I also had to strategize in communication, and craft messages to get buy-in from multiple stakeholders in order to help people understand how participating in inclusion objectives could help everybody reach their goals.

It was really about bridging the gap and finding win-win situations and helping people see the value in initiatives that maybe they didn't consider to be useful at first glance. I also did a lot of work looking at statistics and seeing how initiatives benefited people or increased challenges for them based on their race profile.

This data-driven approach gave weight to the desire to be more inclusive because the evidence was being documented as to what the benefits were. It wasn't just about a feeling, it was about numbers. Being able to quantify progress is a powerful thing and the art of knowing what to measure and how is also really important.

Being able to make a business case for inclusion is key. People want to do the right thing, I believe, but having an understanding of how the right thing can also be the best thing is a great motivator.

Another thing that I found to be really powerful is to break it down to daily activities. We look at deconstructing systems of oppression and smashing the patriarchy, and these are big audacious goals that are valid. But being able to answer "But what does that look like on the ground?" is where the rubber hits the road. Having a big goal can be overwhelming but when you connect what you do on an everyday basis to that big goal, it becomes more manageable.

When I left the federal public service I worried about whether I would get to work on Indigenous projects again, if my work would be meaningful, and if I could make a difference. I ended up working with two nonprofits I really admire that work on inclusion issues and I also spent two years promoting films that shared the social history of Indigenous people.

I created content and helped design campaigns that helped people understand each other. Sharing that social history gives context to why people face the challenges they do, what informs their perspective, and how we can be more sensitive to each other.

My approach to content in my marketing is about creating empathy and understanding between people, building relationships, and finding ways for individuals or groups to meet each other where they are and establishing common ground on which to build. This is the orientation that I bring to my diversity and inclusion work, the idea that our inclusion goals need to be tied to the way we communicate internally and externally.

That commitment to doing better should shine through in the words we choose, the way we describe what we do, and how we relate to our audiences. My life's work sits at the intersection of inclusion and communication: how do we include and talk to each other?

It can't just be about words though, the inclusion piece is key. I've learned you can spend a lot of money attracting people with a message but if their experience doesn't match that then they are going to be repelled, you've wasted money, breached someone's trust, and maybe hurt people along the way.

The goal of *Stay Woke, Not Broke* is to help business owners reach across that gap between laying out the welcome mat and getting ready to invite more people into your world. It's not enough to throw open your doors, you have to be ready to receive.

I am ready to help you welcome more people, foster an inclusive environment, and help more people in more meaningful ways. Are you ready to get inclusive?

1
INTIMATELY INCLUSIVE: A PROFILE OF A COMPANY DOING RIGHT (FOREVER YOURS LINGERIE)

As I was researching for this book, I had the opportunity to interview Sonya Perkins, a business owner I greatly admire. She owns Forever Yours Lingerie in Langley, BC, a size-inclusive, body positive, trans-inclusive, and community-minded business. This is a business that embodies what I think all business owners should be striving for. This was our conversation.

Alison: I love your business and I always have. I see the way that you operate, through size inclusion, which I think is inherently antiracist but also anti-oppressive, and also for all the work that you do in raising funds for ovarian cancer research, for supporting women who are in need and I think those are all great things and that other business owners could really learn a lot from you. What inspired you to set these things in motion for your business? What got you looking to go outside of just selling bras and move into being a community member?

Sonya: I don't think that there was any point where I was like, "OK, I'm going to do this, this is a business decision." When I first started the business, because I'm a plus-size woman, I started out doing just plus sizes. And then after about, I guess, six years of just doing that, we started having more and more and more people wanting to come and be fitted by us because we knew what we were doing and we had a great selection.

It just kind of organically changed over time where I wanted to offer all sizes, because when I go shopping with my girlfriend who, she's a size 10, and I'm a size 18-20, I don't want to have to go to the back corner, where she gets to shop in the middle of the store where it's well lit and pretty, you know, I wanted everybody to be able to come and shop with their friend and so I just tried to be inclusive of what I could find in products and what people actually needed and wanted.

I think it's kind of funny when you see stores now doing this whole big inclusivity campaign, where it's like, "It's a thing, and it's a campaign" and I've been doing this for 25 years, because I just inherently felt that that was the right thing to do. I think that kind of organically changed into doing the other things.

Our bag program came to be because I really want to try and be as environmentally conscious as I can with my business. But at the same time, I'm not in my business to get rich. I have a beautiful house, I have a nice car, we can travel when we want and we aren't uncomfortable. My goal is not to get rich. So rather than saying, "OK, we're going to do this bag program and you're going to not take a bag and [instead of us paying for the bag] we're going to take 50 cents and put it towards a charity that is important to our customers or important to our staff."

One of our models, who I became very close friends with, ended up passing away from ovarian cancer. And so that was something that was really close to my heart. I wanted to do something that was worthwhile and that made me feel like we're doing more than just selling stuff.

I think in retail it can get that it's always about the bottom line. The bottom line is super important, but at the same time, if I'm being paid well and my staff are being paid well and taken care of, and there's still some extra at the end of the year, why shouldn't we be sharing that? Because that as a whole makes our community better and those are my customers that I'm drawing from, they are from our community. For me, it always just became a really organic kind of thing, never really a business decision, which probably is not a great business decision.

Alison: I know, when I started my marketing practice, it was kind of generic and it didn't have any strong positioning or anything. But when I started talking about the things that mattered to me, that's when I started getting more people because they had something to align with.

Sonya: Absolutely, yes. I think I want to be very truthful in my business as well and not sugarcoat it. We all have what we have and we all have insecurities and that's part of the reason why I get on Instagram and show this body, which I'm still working through. I think it's really important for people to realize that we are a real business with real people behind it. We don't care what your body looks like. I have a different body, you have a different body. We're all just women with our own issues. We're here to help people with that.

Alison: I love that. I remember back when one of your suppliers was sending a lot of plastic with their stuff, and you made some purchasing decisions as a result.

Sonya: Yes, the amount of waste that was being generated by those purchases, I quit carrying it, and we didn't carry them for that full season. Obviously, we didn't carry them last year because of the pandemic, but they switched their packaging. They are now sending their swimwear in cloth bags that you can use as a bikini bag that has their logo on it.

My mom always used to say, "Money talks, bullshit walks." I think that is really important for businesses and for retailers to say, "You know what? This doesn't align with my business. And if I'm important to your business and your business's bottom line, then I require you to make some changes." Just like you as a customer can choose where you want to shop, and who you want to shop with because of where your values align, I can do the same with my vendors. If I'm important enough to them dollar-wise, then they start thinking about making changes.

Alison: What is your vision for the future in terms of the impact for your brand and the work that you do?

Sonya: I think my overall vision would be, again, just to have a place where people feel safe and feel comfortable and it's inclusive of genders and sizes. I don't want to have an empire of 50 stores or whatever, I want to keep it small and tight so that I always know that the impact that [we have on people] when they come to us, whether it's shopping in store or online, is that they leave feeling better than when they came in. If we can continue to do that, and continue to support local community things and to support wider national campaigns on important things, both to myself, and my staff and my customers, then that's all I want.

Alison: How have you seen your industry change over time in terms of inclusion and sustainability and kind of overall awareness?

Sonya: There've been huge changes. In terms of inclusion, I think that a lot of the big brands that did the inclusion thing because they were forced to do it and you could tell they were forced to do it. But I think that that's made a huge difference because it's not an uphill battle anymore. When I go to a vendor and say, "Why don't you have 2x? Why don't you have 3x?" They can't really say any more "Oh, nobody wants those sizes." I mean, I've gone to shows in New York, where a vendor will only go up to a large and I'm like, "Seriously? Have you been outside? How did you get here to this trade show this morning? That is not what the average woman is wearing. The fact that you're telling me that, 'Oh, we don't sell that size, it just doesn't work for us,' it's not real."

It's become much easier to get vendors to include sizes because the big guys are doing it. They feel like they have to follow suit. The same thing goes with sustainability because customers are wanting that and also the retailer is wanting that. More and more companies are starting to do it. Everybody needs to keep up with the Joneses. It's a snowball effect. When other companies see companies like [mine] (not to toot my horn at all, that's not what this is), but standing up publicly and saying, "I'm not gonna buy from you," or "Look at the way that this is packaged. This is craziness," they feel safe enough to do the same or to also call that company maybe in private and say, "Hey, you know what, I do hate the way that you package things. It's way too much plastic or it's way too much waste." There's strength in numbers.

It's one thing if it's just me saying to a company, "I don't like this." But if 50 other stores are saying, "I don't like this," they're gonna start doing something about it. So it's the safety of feeling like if somebody has said it first, I can say it next.

Alison: You have a beautiful thriving community of people who love your brand. Have you had any fears or concerns around speaking out on things?

Sonya: I have been really lucky. I think I'm one of those personalities that I just do before I think and then I do it. And then I go, "Oh, what have I done? I jumped not knowing that I could swim!" I've always been like that in business. Sometimes it bites me in the ass. But most of the time, it serves me well, because if I think about it, I'll be too scared to actually do it.

In terms of speaking out about things, I don't really get a whole lot of backlash. Once in a while I do. One of my social media things where I called out a company about their wasteful packaging — the next morning, I had a call from the CEO of the company. I went way up the chain and we talked about different things that their company could do, and they're actually working on changing things.

I've actually been really, really lucky that we, knock on wood, that I don't get a lot of hate at all. I think that people just know that I speak my mind. I want to be respectful of people but I also want to be respectful of the things that are important to me. By hiding them, I don't think that that's respectful of myself for my business.

Alison: Lingerie typically has mostly been, in terms of focus, marketed around women and serving women. I know that you carry menswear that's awesome in stores too. But how does your store look at inclusion for people at various other points on the gender spectrum? What kind of training do your staff have around supporting people who are of different gender identities?

Sonya: Our training is super simple. Our training is you be kind, and you treat every customer just like every customer. You treat them like you would any other customer, and you don't make it a big deal. You treat them kindly and respectfully. You ask them where their boundaries are. If you have boundaries that you're comfortable with, and uncomfortable with, then it's a two-way dance.

Let's say we have somebody who comes in and they are transitioning, and they are presenting as a woman, we will bring them into the women's fitting room, we'll ask them if they feel comfortable being in there. If they don't, we have a private fitting room that we can take them to. If they're presenting as a man, we take them into a separate room, and we present it as a private experience. But we just want to make sure that everybody's treated the same and that nothing really is called out.

We had a customer come in here. This was a few years ago. And he was pregnant, and he was going to give birth soon. Full beard, very handsome man, pregnant belly, and he was here to get nursing bras and he was here with his mom, and they were very nervous about what they were going to expect. Clearly that's not something you see every day, and it could have been an issue and we brought him into the private room.

We treated him like we would have treated any other customer who was coming in for a nursing bra. He and his mom left super happy. She called us about an hour later. She said, "You do not even know what that meant to him to be treated as a regular person who was going to be giving birth and who is going to be having this huge life change and to not have a big deal made of it, and to not have even a comment said about it." This seemed really simple to us, because that's just how we do it. But then it makes you realize what a different life people have, and the different experiences and the hardships that they have in something as simple as buying a nursing bra.

I believe in just treating people like human beings and not treating people necessarily as a gender. If they want to be specifically treated as such, then absolutely, but I just want to treat people as human beings, and I want to use proper pronouns. I want to just treat you like I would want to be treated if I came into [your] shop.

Alison: Something I've always admired is how open you are around conversations around mental health. What was your experience in terms of sharing your journey? Was it something that you consciously thought about whether or not it was a fit for discussing within the context of your business and how has that kind of shifted things for you in your leadership role within your company?

Sonya: I think it's definitely made me a lot more empathetic towards the idea that it's not just physical sick days that people need, some days, you just need a mental day. Some days, you can't stop crying in the morning, and so you can't come to work and you can't do your job well, and it's easier for me to understand that because I go through it. In terms of actually putting it out there, it was never really something, again, that was planned. It was just "Oh, I'm gonna do this. I'm gonna talk about this," because that's what I feel like talking about today.

It was kind of hard putting it out there because I have spent a really solid 20 years hiding it. I never had any kind of depression before I had my son and I ended up having really bad depression during my pregnancy and then really bad postpartum depression, that's kind of when it all kicked off.

It is ridiculously hard to hide it and to always be "on" and to be strong and to have people think that you can carry that load yourself. It finally got to a point where I was like, "I can't do this anymore." I would come to work Monday to Friday, and I would be strong for my team. Everybody thought that I had it together and I was as strong as anybody. Then I would go home and I would get in bed on Friday night, and I wouldn't get out of bed until Sunday evening. And then I would start the cycle all over again.

I needed those two days to just be in my depressive self and not do anything. I finally decided, "You know what? I'm just going to lay it out there. And if I'm having a [bad] day, it's OK to say that you're having a [bad] day." The positive reaction of people going, "You can own a successful business, and you can do good things and you can run a company and you can manage employees, and you can do all that, and you can have a mental illness all at the same time. It's not all or nothing." I didn't realize how important it was for people to see that until I actually put it out there. And that's, I think, why I continue talking about it because it is important to know that it's just not all or nothing. Depressed people can do a lot of stuff and it's not just sitting in your room all day. Exactly.

Alison: How have you approached building an inclusive team? Is that something that you have consciously set out to do within your business? Or has the presence that you put out there just attracted a variety of people?

Sonya: It really has. I think that the more we're out there, and we share what we do and who we are as people, it really makes people want to come and work with us. We have gotten so many really great people over the last few years because they want to be part of what we have going here.

I want different kinds of people. I've made a big point of this, especially in our different departments, because as we're getting bigger, we actually have departments for stuff, it's crazy. That's always one of the things that I'm talking about with our operations director is I want different people, I don't want the same kinds of people in the same department. When people are different, they bring so many different things to the table.

When you're not thinking the same as the person who's working right next to you, you can have those conversations about what's going to work better, and what's going to be better for the company as a whole or for our customers. You're not just stuck in one mindset. I think having people with different life experiences, different age groups, different ethnicities, I think all of those things are really important to bring that scope of experience to the job and to our business.

Alison: Buying intimates can be such an emotional thing, from a trauma perspective, or from a body image recovery kind of perspective and just the whole story of our bodies in terms of why we need a larger or smaller size can be wrapped up in so much stuff. How is that something that you address within your business and the way that you approach customers who are coming in?

Sonya: I think for us and for our fitters, we focus on the fact that it's the garment, it's not you, it's not that your body is wrong, or weird or whatever, it's just that garment doesn't work for your body. And that's OK, because there are a ton of different cuts and there are a ton of different brands, and there are a ton of different styles. Everything is made for different types of bodies. If you're trying to fit into a particular brand that is not going to be right for your body, it's fitting a round peg into a square hole. But we're here to make sure that you find the right thing for you and for your unique body. So we make it more about "It's the garment that's just not working. It's not you."

We work until we find what does work for you and what you feel comfortable in. If you want something sexy, awesome. But lingerie, we have been so brainwashed that it's all about sex, it's all sexy, sexy, sexy. The majority of women that put on a bra in the morning, they're not doing it because they want to feel sexy, they're doing it because that's just what you do in the Western world. We want to just make sure that people are OK with that and we know that we can get you something sexy, but we can also get you something basic that's just going to take you through your day and whatever you want.

We also talked about inclusion and what it means from a small-business owner's perspective. Here's what Sonya had to say:

Sonya: I think it's just so important that people really find something that means something to them, and that they're passionate about. I see it so often on social media, where you can see when people are not being authentic, and they're just doing something because they think it's going to enhance their business or increase sales or whatever the case may be. I think that it's so transparent when that happens. Maybe some of the big guys that can hire marketing companies can make it look seamless. But so often you see where it's just not, or it's a one off that happens once in a while, and then nothing else happens.

We have one particular brand, it's a women's line of lingerie, but they do a lot of photos of men who enjoy wearing it. We'll post those photos, not saying anything, just like we would post a picture of a woman in that outfit. And sometimes I post it and think, oh, I can't wait to see what I'm going to get on that. And there's nothing. Because we're not making a big deal out of it. We're just like, this is a product that we carry, we post it on women. And here's a man wearing it. It's just people who wear it.

Sonya also shared her experiences with the speed of social media as a small-business owner.

Sonya: I think with social media, it's hard, especially with small businesses, because everybody wants you to have a say on everything. Sometimes you don't know what to say or how to say it. Even if you take a day or two to think about, "How do I want to address this?" It's too long. It's really hard nowadays with social media and everybody wanting everything to be instant, that you can't even sometimes have a minute to think about, "As a white person, how do I address this?" Because I don't know anything about it. "How do I respectfully and empathetically address it without sounding like a bandwagon jumper?"

Forever Yours Lingerie is a business that I am constantly inspired by personally and professionally. I have been a customer for years because beyond being incredibly ethical, they are also really good at what they do. They are experts at finding the right fit for bras and lingerie, and a leader in helping people feel like they fit in their business.

2
KEY TERMS DEFINED

If we are going to have a conversation about social justice and business, it's important to use common language. A wide variance in definitions could mean that we misunderstand each other so I want to be clear up front about my working definitions of the key terms you will find in this book.

What Is Social Justice?

Dictionary.com's definition of social justice is this: Fair treatment of all people in a society, including respect for the rights of minorities and equitable distribution of resources among members of a community. For me, it's about equitable access to resources, opportunities, representation, and justice within a society.

There's nuance in this categorization. From my perspective, it's acknowledging that access to the legal system and access to justice are not necessarily the same thing. I think about accessibility in terms of how meaningful it is. I used to work in a building that had an accessible washroom stall but no access button to get into the bathroom. It's only accessible if you can access the accommodation and there was a barrier to doing that.

When I talk about social justice I am talking not about the appearance of equity and going through the motions of inclusion and issuing statements about world issues because that's what's expected. I believe in meaningful action that actually makes a difference. Making statements is important and being clear about where you stand matters, but what you do about it matters even more.

Social justice is about righting wrongs, dismantling oppressive power structures, and behaving ethically in our interactions, initiatives, and communications. It's inherently about respecting other people and doing the right thing. It's about doing the right thing not just because it's popular or trendy, but because it's in alignment with who you are and you genuinely care about what happens to people.

It's about recognizing and taking apart systemic barriers and finding ways for things to be fair and for people to be able to enjoy their lives safely, generate what they need to live, and enjoy the same things everyone else does without being penalized or oppressed because of sexism, racism, ableism, homophobia, or transphobia.

What Is an Intersectional Perspective and Why Is It Important?

When I talk about having an intersectional perspective, I'm talking about having a perspective that acknowledges and understands the intersection points between various identities. It is a perspective that looks critically at an issue that affects people from one identity and looks at how it also affects people of other or multiple identities.

As an example, feminism acknowledges the gender pay gap, where intersectional feminism acknowledges that that gap is greater for women of color, and for women with disabilities, and that because of toxic masculinity that can influence this situation, people of other gender identities may also face discrimination that results in inequitable pay.

An intersectional perspective is holistic and considers an issue from multiple angles and experiences, and understands that the bolstering of gender-based outcomes that doesn't also support the advancement of racialized people isn't good enough. It's not enough to address the gender pay gap by ensuring white women make as much as their male counterparts. It also needs to ensure that Black women make as much as their white male counterparts (or even their white female counterparts).

An intersectional perspective doesn't impose a gender binary and it also acknowledges that people belong to many cultures and may identify with a variety of experiences based on what has happened in their lives. It's a more expansive way of looking at social issues and it gives the opportunity for conversations of greater depth and nuance.

What Is Decolonization?

Decolonization is often talked about in terms of removing colonial structures. On the Queen's University website for their Centre for Teaching and Learning they talk about a parallel process of Indigenization, meaning adding Indigenous properties to a process or a structure (www.queensu.ca/ctl/resources/decolonizing-and-indigenizing/what-decolonization-what-indigenization, accessed November 2021). Typically, decolonization is discussed in terms of Indigenous and non-Indigenous people and about restructuring the institutions that Indigenous people need to navigate.

An example of a colonial structure that could be addressed through decolonization is looking at an institution's definition of family in policy. In a colonist structure, that definition might look like immediate family members of a nuclear family and be quite rigid. When we look at family from an Indigenous perspective, the definition could be a lot more broad. When you consider the role of the extended family in raising a child, or the presence of a multigenerational household, the scope of family could be much more expansive in other cultural contexts.

One way that I encountered this was when trying to get leave for the funeral of a family member. The colonist structure decided that "nephew" wasn't important enough to qualify for bereavement leave, but I was welcome to take vacation time. The reality is, often these colonial structures don't even meet the needs or respect the life experience of people with more "normative" identities. A white person would be impacted by the death of the child of their sibling also, it's not just in the expanded cultural definition where there is a barrier.

Often, colonial structures are more restrictive generally, but that comes from the worldview it is based on and what is valued and what is believed to be true about the people operating within the system. Decolonizing involves looking at the ways of being of an organization and looking at the rules and regulations, policies, and practices and seeing from where they originate.

Colonization was a historical event where Indigenous people were overtaken by an outside force and where they had new structures imposed on them that didn't serve them and actively oppressed them. In Canada, this looked like the pass system, the chief and council structure, the residential school system, the child welfare system, and the prison system. It also presented as colonial justice structures that were incompatible with Indigenous justice practices or perspectives.

We talk about this in a historical context, but there are still examples of colonization today. Colonial attitudes were present during the pandemic where people traveled to vacation places where Indigenous people were more vulnerable. They brought with them risk of infection and risk of needing to access what few resources were available to the locals, without adding to those resources. Similarly, a high-profile couple traveled to the North to access vaccines intended for people in a vulnerable location. These are colonizing practices where the needs and realities of local people are sacrificed for the wants of people who aren't from there.

Decolonization is a worthy goal, but should be approached also with an Indigenization practice to bring back balance and to make the institutions, structures, and processes that Indigenous people navigate more reflective of their worldviews and experiences, and more respectful of their needs.

What Is White Privilege?

White privilege is a form of privilege afforded by white supremacy. While it doesn't mean that you didn't earn everything you've achieved or gained as a white person, or that you haven't faced trials or barriers, it does mean that you haven't faced additional barriers because you are white.

When you see news headlines that talk about a retired Black judge being arrested on an evening walk because he "fit a profile" or a Black realtor being arrested at a showing because someone thought he was breaking in, these are the sorts of experiences that white people typically don't have to experience or endure because white privilege provides the assumption of safety.

Gina Crossley-Corcoran wrote an article called "Explaining White Privilege To A Broke White Person" which is often cited and referenced (theavarnagroup.com/resources/explaining-white-privilege-to-a-broke-white-person, accessed November 2021). The thrust of her piece is that while white privilege exists, intersectionality lets us look at the ways we experience privilege and the ways we struggle based on other identity intersection points.

White privilege, or any form of privilege, is important to consider if you are evaluating the validity of a complaint about a barrier or accessibility issue. Just because something isn't a problem for you doesn't mean it isn't a problem. Being aware of privilege means that you can be cognizant of where your identity mitigates challenges in ways others don't have the same experience.

This is particularly true when making claims around income and success rates of programs. If you find that the majority of the participants that do well share common characteristics, it's valid to question if what is being taught is enough to improve likelihood for success for anyone or if it's more likely to be limited to people who have predispositions to positive outcomes by virtue of proximity, familiarity, and an absence of bias.

White privilege is something to be aware of when making decisions as a business owner and when thinking about how you implement social justice within your business. Privilege gives you the opportunity to lift up others and pass the mic. It isn't something you need to feel guilty about, it's something you can use to help make change in the world.

What Is Purpose Washing?

Purpose washing is when you use a cause to sell merchandise when a direct donation would be more effective or when your involvement in the cause is suspect. It's performative activism (activism done for the sake of optics with little impact), or slacktivism (low-effort, low-impact activism activities) that is commercially motivated, generally shortsighted, and may contain elements of virtue signaling (acting or speaking to look virtuous or morally right).

These activities are typically undertaken in order to give off the appearance of doing the right thing when in actual fact the level of effort is minimal and the actions undertaken might actually have an opposite effect. Often, so little thought has gone into things that the possible impact is hard to quantify.

This is why it's so important to partner with people who are actually doing the work so that if you want to make an impact, you can implement solutions that make sense and are going to be helpful to people. Listen to the advice of those who are active in the area that you want to support and know the best way to lend a hand.

Purpose washing is something that is often seen in terms of breast cancer which is referred to as pinkwashing, or among corporations during pride month or Black History Month. Ultimately, if you actually care about a community, you need to be actively engaged in discussing their issues all year round and not just when everybody else is talking about it and it's trendy.

It's kind of like Mother's Day, if you treat your mother badly all year long but you give her a nice card on Mother's Day, is that a relationship that you would be proud of? Will anybody take your claims seriously if you only do it once a year when it's expected? This is why content planning is so crucial so that you can sustain interest and ongoing relevant conversations throughout the year. We will talk more about content later on in this book.

If you were designing special packaging in order to celebrate an awareness day, and in doing so creating waste and operating in a way that's less sustainable, it's valid to question how thoughtful the gesture was.

Purpose washing is something that is generally raised when there seems to be a disconnect between your everyday activities and your acts of activism. If people know to expect activism and organization from you, it won't be as questionable as when it's from somebody who generally doesn't participate but is selling something with a view to giving to a cause that they generally haven't been connected to. It looks like they're just trying to make more sales by aligning themselves with a popular cause and hoping that people will be encouraged to make purchases they wouldn't already, and that profit is being generated off of the backs of tragedies and misfortunes. This is common in breast cancer fundraising, where pink items are purchased with very small amounts of proceeds going to actual research.

Ultimately, people don't want to be manipulated and they don't want to be misled. They want to be part of something that is meaningful and they don't like being tricked into feeling like they're making a difference when they aren't really, or when their sympathies are being played on for the purpose of making a buck.

What Is a Marginalized Identity?

It used to be that we talked about people from marginalized identities as minorities, but that was language that was very white-centered. More recent language looks to categorize these groups as the global majority because the majority of the world's population isn't white.

Marginalized identities aren't just non-white people, they also include people that are not heterosexual, who are women, or who don't fit within the traditional gender binary, who have disabilities, or anyone who doesn't fit within the norms.

When I talk about groups of people who have faced barriers based on their race, gender, sexual orientation, or level of ability, I use the words "historically excluded" instead of "marginalized" or "underrepresented." I do that because "underrepresented" is the net outcome, but using language like "historically excluded" puts the focus on why people aren't represented — because over time they have been consciously left out.

When we focus on what led to the current situation, we can better address the solution. If someone has been historically excluded, it's time to start including them. When we focus on the outcome, "underrepresented," we can spend a lot of time postulating as to why that is. "Maybe they just aren't interested," "maybe they don't have that capacity," "maybe they have other opportunities," "maybe they don't want to be included," and we can wring our hands and say "it's very sad that these folks aren't at the table, but what are we to do if they don't want to come? "

By focusing on the behavior instead of the outcome, we can design solutions that address it. In what ways can historical exclusion be addressed? These are some ideas:

- Targeted outreach
- Mentorship
- Scholarship
- Internships
- Strategic recruitment
- Changes in advertising tactics to be seen where the target market actually spends time
- Internal policy changes to become an employer of choice

If you don't know how to include people, reach out to experts who can help. Hire a reputable diversity, equity, and inclusion consultant in your area to help you navigate these issues. Take the time to read content produced by the consultants to see what their approach to diversity is and if it aligns with your values. Google is your friend but also ask other people in your network if they can recommend someone. You don't get extra diversity and inclusion points by figuring it out yourself. When you know that diverse businesses make more money and your business isn't diverse, all the time you spend perpetuating historical exclusion is costing your business money you could be making if you had the right people around the table. There is an opportunity cost that comes with complacency.

I always say that it isn't about songs of love and light, it's about getting the right people around the campfire. When people are historically excluded and that is allowed to continue, you aren't getting the best talent, you're getting the best talent that is part of the normative identity. You aren't getting the best solutions, you're getting the best solutions a bunch of people with the same background can come up with.

What Is Cancel Culture?

Cancel culture is something that happens when someone does something that does not seem to be equitable, or behaves in an egregious manner that goes against a group's norms and expectations around how one conducts oneself. Often, when somebody says or does something questionable, there will be a lot of outrage, usually displayed online.

That outrage can feel overwhelming and the consequences of whatever choice that was made can result in a loss of funds or reputation or standing within a community. When people lose out on things that they would normally expect to receive there can be a lot of language used around cancel culture.

A lot of business owners come to me wanting to talk about how to navigate social issues and avoid cancel culture. Certainly there are people who genuinely want to do the right thing and are misinformed and make choices they would ultimately regret. The accountability for their actions can feel painful and shameful. The financial costs could be devastating especially if the situation isn't handled well in the beginning.

There isn't a secret "get out of cancel culture free" card but you can make an effort to educate yourself, to listen to your audience, to engage with experts, and do your best to do the right thing. There are certainly examples where people have faced disproportionate consequences for infractions and these are held up as examples of the irrational, unwavering left.

Some examples of cancel culture are simply examples of social consequences of unpopular or uninformed choices. These are examples of accountability and social sanctions. Sometimes when somebody is feeling resentful about social consequences or financial consequences that come from accountability it gets conflated with cancel culture when it is really not to that extent.

There will be people who will be unreasonable, who you will never be able to satisfy in terms of moral perfectionism and the standards that they have for you. There will be people who feel there's only one way to handle something and that if you don't do exactly what they would have done, that you are wrong. The customer or the audience member is not always right but even someone who is seeming to be unreasonable or disproportionate can have an impact on the opinions of other people.

That doesn't mean it's not worth striving toward doing better, though it does mean that there needs to be a balance of expectations around how you conduct yourself and an awareness that nobody can know everything and that all you can do is the best you can. This should be an inspiration toward ongoing quality improvement and not a hall pass for complacency. It's not about complacency, it's about not subscribing to moral perfectionism.

Coming back and healing that relationship with your audience is something to be done with intention and thoughtfulness. Later on we will talk about how to apologize and the best way to make reparations. For now, focus on not letting the fear of cancel culture get in the way of making strides toward your inclusion goals.

There can be a vulnerability when you say that you want to be inclusive because there's this fear that people will be judging you and telling you that you're doing it wrong or that you're not doing it enough. It can be hard to open up for yourself to that kind of criticism when you only want to do the right thing. The threat of cancel culture looming can amplify that even more.

If you can concentrate on all of the times that you have solved problems in your business, repaired relationships, and come together with other stakeholders to find a solution, you can feel confident about your ability to navigate conflict in your journey towards social justice integration within your business.

If you are running a business, you have the skills that you need in order to embark on this journey. There are things that you will need to learn along the way but don't feel like you can't do this because you can, absolutely. Whenever you're developing a new way of doing something you consult, you research, you develop processes and workflows, you think through the benchmarks for success, and you look at the risks of what you are undertaking.

The same goes for integrating a new value in your business that you plan to discuss with the public. If you approach it in a very similar way from a place of systems, you are better positioned to be able to handle challenges in implementation as they come up. Cancel culture is out there but there are also resources, allies, communities, and opportunities to do good.

3
DOES SOCIAL JUSTICE BELONG IN BUSINESS?

Whether social justice belongs in business is a point of contention. Some people believe that values and politics should be private. Others are skeptical about companies that want to do good for the sake of doing good. It is understandable for a CEO to want to be involved in shaping legislation or social attitudes that impact their company's bottom line. After all, companies exist to make money and it is a CEO's job to lead with that goal in mind.

When activism branches off from industry-specific or revenue-generating goals, that's where conversations can get a bit dicey around who has a genuine interest or who has a horse in the race, so to speak. Increasing social justice can have downstream benefits that can be long-term investments for a company, but sometimes those benefits can be very downstream.

Corporate Social Responsibility: Real Impact or Posing?

A recent documentary, *The New Corporation* (Abbot & Bakan, 2020), addresses the pledges of being focused on the triple bottom line that are made by CEOs and interrogates how effective and authentic they really are. It's understandable to be skeptical. On the heels of the confirmation of hundreds of Indigenous children's graves across North America, many businesses made statements of support and concern. Not too long after, Canada Day rolled around.

How do you handle a celebration of a colonial structure — the country called Canada — just weeks after mourning the impacts of colonization? There is a need for activism to have internal cohesion. It should make sense in its entirety and not just be seemingly disconnected, feel-good pieces. They should ideally be based on an ideology and have internal checks and balances to address things that seem inconsistent. For example, a social media post describing sorrow over the graves and then a Canada Day sale the next day might seem in poor taste. Your promotional content should be consistent with the values that you have shared.

Diversity, Equity, and Inclusion (DEI) Activities

The reality is that humans are messy. We are often guided by our hearts, and without a cohesive strategy to look at actions related to diversity, equity, inclusion (DEI), and social justice, you may end up looking like you're going off on tangents and that your activism activities are at odds with each other.

Strategy in your DEI activities

This comes down to the difference between initiatives and strategy. Strategy is salad like initiatives are vegetables. Salad is made up of vegetables, but vegetables on their own are not salads. Salad is the layering and combination of the ingredients to create a cohesive dish. That's how you can have initiatives: Good-for-you activities that are like vegetables for your business, but without a cohesive plan, it's not a salad.

Where diversity, equity, and inclusion efforts can go wrong

Not having a strategy is one way diversity, equity, and inclusion (DEI) efforts can go wrong. Other ways they can go wrong is when they aren't authentically embraced by those responsible, when they aren't delegated or integrated into daily life, when it's done in silos without cross-discipline collaboration — and also when it isn't discussed or shared. A lot of brand journalism opportunities are missed when there isn't adequate discussion about the impactful activities that are taking place. Brand journalism is talking about what your brand is up to and doing it in a way that is outside of traditional press releases; it's taking your brand's stories and turning them into blogs or other types of content.

This isn't to say that activities should be undertaken so they can be viewed in public for optics' sake. If you are going to go to the effort to make your business more inclusive, and if you are going to innovate and create things that you're proud of, talking about those things in public is going to help you draw in more people who are in alignment with your values.

Bringing DEI front and center

The impact of talking about the work that you do to create diversity, equity, and inclusion in your workplace could look like:

- Being able to reach your hiring goals.
- Attracting more people who hold values consistent with your corporate culture.
- Opportunities to collaborate with other brands.
- An ability to influence best practices across your industry.
- Positioning yourself as a more ethical choice in the market for consumers.

When you are able to attract a broader range of employees with a wider span of life experiences, you have a better ability to solve solutions. Research has also shown that more diverse companies make more money. Positive psychology has demonstrated that happy employees are more productive employees and job satisfaction is a component of employee happiness, as well as a sense of belonging and significance.

The DEI advantage

When you put diversity to work in your business in a meaningful way, people start to feel like they belong, like their contributions matter, and like the work they do makes a difference. When there's skepticism and the initiatives aren't being undertaken with transparency or seem to be lip service, people become demoralized and disengaged. They check out and move on.

Corporate social responsibility, the integration of social justice in your business and the act of embracing diversity, equity, and inclusion are ways to engage your employees and avoid presenteeism (when people come to work but don't accomplish much and aren't involved).

With the remote work of the COVID-19 pandemic expanding employee options for employment, you need to position yourself to attract the best talent. If you can draw from talent from anywhere, because you allow remote work, you may find that you recruit people who are very different from the people you could recruit within your home community.

Integrating DEI into your business practices helps you better retain those new hires because the workplace has been readied for their arrival. When your managers and team members are equipped to have more positive interactions and collaborations with people who are different from them, there is more opportunity to create new solutions and a lower risk of harm from placing an employee from a historically excluded community into a workplace that isn't accepting or interested in working together.

Inclusive Leadership Qualities

If you want to be a leader in inclusion within your business, these are some qualities you are going to want to nurture within yourself and your team:

- **Adaptability:** You need to be able to change with the times and shift out of "the way we have always done things." Willingness to do things differently is important for developing an inclusive workplace. There's no sense bringing more perspectives to the table if you aren't willing to transform how you do business based on the insights that come from your team.

- **Antifragility:** This is a word that means that you can take feedback without breaking. You can be strong enough to hear things that you might not want to listen to. You can accept a dissenting opinion, and you can try and learn from it. One of the ways to increase your antifragility is having a growth mindset. That's about taking what you know, learning more things, being open to the process, and accepting that learning as constant quality improvement, and not getting discouraged about how there's always more things to learn or feeling like a failure when you get it wrong.

- **Approachability:** Your community needs to be able to come to you and speak to you about challenges. They need to feel like it's a safe place to provide feedback. You need transparency, to be able to be clear about what is important to you, what your expectations are, and what people can expect from you.

- **Bravery:** It's a brave thing to make a decision to be inclusive. It's stepping out of the status quo. It's about trying new things. It's about opening yourself up to criticism. It's a really brave decision to stand up for people.

- **Coachability:** Nobody wants to teach someone who is committed to not learning. You need to be willing to accept feedback and learn from others. Being coachable is what empowers people to coach you. There's nothing more frustrating that being the advisor to someone who doesn't want to be advised.

- **Commitment:** We need to commit to the journey of inclusion because it isn't something that happens overnight. It takes work, and it can be hard work, but it's really worth it. The best way to not look like a bandwagon jumper is to stick with the wagon. Stay the course and continue to reap the rewards of building an inclusive business.

- **Compassion:** This is a trait that is important not just for others, but also for ourselves. We are all learning and we need to have compassion for ourselves, that we may not get things right the first time but that we're going to keep trying.

- **Curiosity:** Being curious is important. When we're limited by our own worldview, we have to get really curious about what other people are experiencing. It's the old expression that a fish can't see the water around it. That's the environment. We have to get really curious in order to learn more about what other people are experiencing.

- **Empathy:** People need to know that you care how they feel, you've been able to put yourself in their shoes, and you've considered why they might be feeling the way they're feeling, so that they can share their feelings with you.

- **Innovation:** The ability to innovate is important for finding new solutions and new ways to do things together when the status quo isn't working. We need to be able to look at new ways that we can welcome people, new ways we can serve people, and new ways we can support people's learning.

- **Self-care:** This is a long-term commitment, and you can tire yourself out trying to do all the things without enough resources in the beginning as you're learning. You need to take care of yourself so that you don't burn out and so that you can keep showing up for your community in the way that you would like.

- **Vision:** You need a vision for inclusion, you need to know what inclusion looks like in your business, and what you would like it to look like, and where you're headed. That vision can help inspire your team, your clients, and it gives you a direction to move in. If you don't know where you're going, you will never know when you get there. You can integrate that vision into your diversity statement.

- **Willingness to learn:** We need to be willing to grow, to gather more information, and to go through the learning process that might be uncomfortable because it's growth and it's change. Being willing to go through that process is important for being an inclusive leader.

4
THE LANGUAGE OF INCLUSION

How to Use Words of Welcome to Include More People

The words that we use to welcome people can have a big impact on whether they actually feel welcome. Language evolves over time, and so does the way in which people want to be referred. There's a lot of nuance in language and sometimes we will select words thinking that we are being inclusive when what we are actually doing is the opposite.

Obviously, our intent matters but our impact is what guides people in their decision to purchase, follow, or align themselves with our brand. We can have the best of intentions but if the words we use are harmful, then it won't change the end result. Intentions are important context around decisions but we have to be aware that those intentions don't necessarily mitigate the amount of harm that we can do unintentionally.

One example of this is the word "womxn." Originally conceived to separate the root of "men" from a word used to describe another gender, over time it also evolved into a way that people used to signal whether they included trans or nonbinary people within their definition of women (if they served women). While it was initially, in some circles, seen to be a positive thing, ultimately many trans women felt that the use of the x when talking about groups that included them meant that the business owner didn't feel like they were "real women."

It was seen to be performative because if someone believes that trans women are women then why would they need to use a different word to describe them? There was a sense that there was a separation that was being created and that their identity was being put in quotation marks rather than being accepted as fact.

Another similar expression that is used to include people from a variety of identities is "participants of all gender identities are welcome so long as they are comfortable in spaces that center the experiences of women." It is well-intended but the way it can be received is that people of different gender identities are welcome as long as they understand that they need to be quiet.

Their contribution is identified to be of less value or importance and that they will not be equal contributors to the conversation because the focus is on people who are not them. They will not be excluded, they just will not be served in the same way. This is seen by some to be a trans-exclusionary radical feminist dog whistle even though it is often used by people who don't necessarily align with those values.

Too often when we develop language for policy and marketing, we look at words that other people use and adopt it because we feel it is the standard and people will know what it means. On the surface, language can be well-intended but still exclusionary. There are a lot of resources out there to help you find the right words. There are style guides you can find that deal with how to talk about different groups of people or how to write from a perspective that honors diversity. Google "style guide" and the subject you are looking to write about to find what is available.

Racial Issues in Language

When we look at the words we use, it is really important to think about racially coded language. Thinking about things like blacklisting something or whitelisting something (blacklisting as a negative thing, versus whitelisting as a positive thing).

It's also important to be aware of privilege when you're selecting your language for your content. One example of this is the word "bulletproof." It might be something that you use to convey that something is solid and indestructible — maybe conceptually, maybe literally — but when you use that, with an audience of people who have been subjected to police shootings, think about how they would love to be "bulletproof." Using words like that without considering the associated trauma can be really upsetting, problematic, and distracting. It distracts from your message. Be aware of people's relationships with the words that you use and be mindful of that.

Even some slang that we typically use that we don't mean to be offensive can have racist roots.

A powwow is a ceremony and a cultural event and we often use it interchangeably with meeting, gathering, or event. Talking about "the low man on the totem pole" could be more sensitively expressed as "entry-level employee." "Savage" is something that gets used a lot in pop culture. The reality of that word is that it's essentially the N word, but for Indigenous people. It's a word that was used to justify atrocities for a lot of years. The word "tribe" can be really problematic. Regardless of how you feel about whether that's a valid concern, it's important to consider, do you want that distraction from your message? If you can use a different word that isn't charged in the same way, why wouldn't you? As an Indigenous person, when I hear the term "tribe" I think about the racism that I've experienced in my life. I think about how people have made being tribal to be something that is negative and undesirable. But now it's trendy to refer to your group of people as a tribe?

Any kind of casual reference to Pocahontas should be avoided. There may have been a Disney movie, but Pocahontas was a real person who experienced some tragic things. Using that lightly can be really upsetting because it's exploitative of the memory of a real person who was significantly impacted by colonization.

Ableist Issues in Language

Avoid ableist language. You might describe something as uninteresting or boring instead of "lame," which refers to people with mobility challenges. "Crazy" is another one to try and remove from your content. People who struggle with mental health challenges who have been stigmatized by that might not appreciate that word. Other words you could use could be wild or surprising. "Tone deaf" can be difficult for people with hearing impairment, you might consider instead "lacking in situational awareness."

When you talk about someone being "blind" to something, other language you might consider could be around not having awareness of something, or not having a perspective that includes that.

Developing a Style Guide for Your Business

Style guides are documents that outline what is acceptable language to use when discussing an issue and also what language should be avoided. These are guardrails for your communication to keep the conversation on a predetermined track.

There are style guides about specific identities that talk about the best language to use and why and what the standard current language is because that can change over time. Typically, these are developed by experts in the field and they are kept current based on changing standards, trends, and norms.

Having a style guide in place is a good way to standardize the way you talk about who you are, who you serve, and what you do in a way that includes more people. You can develop these guides in consultation with a consultant, by holding a focus group, and in reviewing other style guides and thought leadership pieces in your field.

If we are looking at things from a gendered perspective, these are some questions to ask yourself as you develop your style guide:

- When you look at your communications and the way you talk about what you do, is there an assumption of gender and is it intentional or has it evolved from a habit of the way you talk about people?

- Do you actually only serve one gender or do you serve people from a variety of gender identities though most often people of one gender identity?

- Are you open to serving people of different identities and do you want that to be showcased in the language that you use?

- Is the activity, approach, or philosophy something that is gendered?

An example of a business that has been deliberately gender-inclusive is a company called Aisle and it manufactures menstrual products. It uses language to describe their customers as the people who menstruate versus the traditional language of menstrual products which centers around women's identities. Aisle recognizes that trans men menstruate and nonbinary people menstruate. It adjusts language accordingly so that people know that they make a product that meets their needs and it is intentional about how it describes people, because the company acknowledges that menstruation isn't something that has to be centered around a specific gender identity. Communicating in a way that implies that it does is actually harmful.

Another example would be within the birth industry where the default might speak to the person who is delivering the baby from the perspective of motherhood; the language that could be used to be more inclusive could be the "birthing parent." You don't technically need to be a mother to give birth and communication that normalizes that people of varying identities give birth is more inclusive.

Focusing on the gendered title of "mother" may give people the impression that you are not equipped to serve birthing parents who are not planning to identify as mothers and or that you do not acknowledge the validity of their identity in relation to the life stage on which they are embarking.

Go through the language that you use to talk about who you are, what you do, and who you serve on your website (or wherever that language may be) and see if there are assumptions that you are making about your customers. Interrogate whether those assumptions are true. Think about whether there are people who might look at the language that you use and wonder if you are able to serve them.

It's one thing to want to include a variety of people but it's another thing to be equipped to do so. Find out what the needs are for the population that you don't currently serve and see if those are needs that you can meet. If you can't personally meet those needs, consider bringing in somebody who can, to be able to service those clients and think about the best way that you can accommodate people that you are hoping to attract with your updated inclusive language.

From a technical perspective, a style guide should talk about how you habitually refer to people, why the language is used, and also identify what terms are not acceptable so that people understand how to talk about what you do, who you serve, and who you are. This way there is less margin for error. Essentially, creating your style guide enables you to create policy that sets expectations about how people are included from a language perspective. Setting out the expectations in advance gives people guidance so they don't accidentally exclude people.

For more information consult our downloadable forms kit, accessible through the URL printed at the back of this book.

Why You Need a Diversity Statement

There are a number of reasons why having a diversity statement is important for your website. A diversity statement is a piece of copy that talks about what you believe in and what you stand for in terms of diversity, and what that looks like in practice.

When you make a diversity statement you're supporting purchasing decisions, clarifying your position, making a public commitment, qualifying leads, and leveraging your platform for good. Here's why all of this is important:

- **Supports purchasing decisions:** The reason why I always suggest a diversity statement, or one of the reasons anyway, is that there are a lot of people who make purchasing decisions based on the presence of a diversity statement. Do I know where this company stands? Does this company care about me? People are more likely to spend money with companies with whom their values align and when they support where their money is going.

  Values can drive whether people decide to do business with you. This is why some people don't shop at Hobby Lobby or Chick-fil-A; there are specific values those businesses are known for and people who aren't aligned with them make other purchasing decisions that are more in line with their values.

- **Clarity of position:** A diversity statement is more than just a piece of web copy. It really should be a guiding light and a signal to people that you're a safe space, that you actually do genuinely care about them. It supports better relationships with your staff, and with your customers because it helps people know where you stand. A diversity statement helps people get to know you and what you're about, who you are as a business owner, and what your life is like.

  Last year there was a list that was compiled and it included all of the major tech companies, whether or not they've made a statement about BLM, what it was, how much money they make, how many employees they have, how many of them are Black. It really took a critical look at what people were saying versus what people were doing and how closely they matched up.

- **Public commitment:** Having a diversity statement makes your position and commitment known to the public. It's a social risk because you're telling people that you care about something. Doing that is going to call in the people who care about what you care about and invite them on your journey to do good together. That public commitment can also let clients not aligned with your values know where you stand to help them decide if a collaboration makes sense for their brand or personal beliefs.

- **Qualifying leads:** There's a risk when you tell people what you care about that they won't care about it, too. There will be people who don't agree with your position or think you shouldn't have one. But it lets you consciously let people choose you because they are excited by what you are about and it helps you not work with people who are not aligned with you.

When you make a position, there will be people who oppose it. That's not always a bad thing. You may not enjoy working with people who are not aligned with your values either. It's not just the customer who's making a choice. It's also you; you get to choose.

- **Leverage your platform for good:** A diversity statement lets you use your communications asset (such as your website) to start making change in the world and by mobilizing your audience. It lets you use something you've developed for one purpose and give it another job. It makes your website multifunctional, selling your audience into what you do and what you believe in.

Ultimately, if you care about something deep in your heart, why wouldn't you want people to know about that? Be brave enough to say what you stand for and let your people show up.

How to Create a Diversity Statement

Now that you know why you need a diversity statement, here's what you need to know about what that should look like from an implementation perspective.

Your diversity statement should have some key components Some large brands have statements as short as 25 words. I recommend a lot more detail than that.

Components of a diversity statement

1. **Accessibility:** The first component of a diversity statement is that it needs to be accessible. People need to be able to read it. A variety of people with different backgrounds need to be able to understand what you mean. Consider the education level of your target audiences and use a reading level assessment tool online to see how legible it is. If your statement is going to be image-based, make sure to use alt-text with a detailed image description so that people who use screen readers will know what your graphic says.

   If you're going to do a video or audio instead of copy, you're going to want to make sure that you include a transcript or written copy for people who are hearing impaired, Deaf, or are not auditory learners. There's nothing more embarrassing than when somebody with a disability can't access your Inclusion Statement. That's a sign that inclusion is still an area that you need to work on.

   Captions and video make content more accessible, but when they're auto generated, often they're referred to as "craptions" because they're notoriously inaccurate. Get a real human to help you or a service so that your caption quality is good. Some machine transcription can also really struggle with anything that isn't an American accent. If you're going to use captions, make sure they're helpful.

2. **Consistency:** Your diversity statement should be consistent with the rest of the copy on your website and in any other places you have written information so that people will know it's from you. They will know you've put thought into it, recognize the language as being familiar to the way that you normally show up for your people, and know that it's genuine. It's not a template that you bought where you filled in the boxes. This is your brand voice with your brand message.

3. **Connection:** Your diversity statement should be connected to your vision and values. How does your diversity vision contribute to the overall vision of your company and the

values of your company? If you've done the work around these areas, those are good connecting pieces to consider.

Think about your company's vision and values: How is having diversity and inclusion in your business contributing to that? How does being inclusive support the goals that your company has? You want people to know that it's so important to you that you've connected it to being core to your business.

4. **Cohesion with company culture:** Your values around diversity and inclusion should be integrated into the culture of your organization. That means it's not just lip service, you've been able to connect the dots between the copy that's on your website and elsewhere and how you operate in the world, and that is reflected in the way your company does everything.

5. **Specificity:** Your diversity statement needs to answer some key questions: who, how, which, why, and where? You want to be specific about who you are including. Are you including people based on race, on ability, or gender, sexual orientation? Are there areas that you prioritize?

It's about more than having a feeling that you want to include people. It's about really looking at the practices of your business, the reality of your business, what you're capable of doing, the customer experience, and the extent to which those things reflect that you are inclusive. A diversity statement is more than a mission statement about inclusion, it's a critical evaluation of how you show up for your customers or your readers.

Be clear about how you include people and include that in your statement. Do you have inclusive policies? Do you have employee groups that are geared towards the demographic you're looking to support? How have you built infrastructure to support people from different backgrounds? What are your payment policies?

If you have addressed any historical policies and made changes to make your business more inclusive, talk about that. Also look at your charitable giving, including questions such as:

- Which causes does your company support and how?

- How do you encourage your employees to give?
- Do they take a volunteer day every year or every quarter?
- Do you make monetary donations?
- If so, what percentage of your revenue are you donating?

Look at who you're donating to and why you picked them. Being clear about that creates trust and accountability. And people can ask more questions like, what are you doing? How are you actually supporting these causes?

When you get clear about how you give back, you can talk about the causes that are important to you in more concrete ways. If you're addressing poverty, and giving to poverty related charities, you're addressing something that is often associated with experiences around race, around gender. There are many different features that people are discriminated against and that impacts their bottom line. When you target poverty you're supporting people who have been discriminated against.

You might say "We target our social justice efforts on alleviating poverty. We acknowledge that people of color, women, that any number of groups face systemic barriers — to wealth building, to food security, to income security — and our brand is taking these actions in order to address these things. We acknowledge that there are people who are specifically more at risk of experiencing poverty by virtue of racism or virtue of sexism, by virtue of homophobia, or any number of factors that can influence somebody from not being promoted, not being hired, not being able to access credit, not being able to access housing. All of those things feed into the experience of poverty and can be influenced by all sorts of intersectional factors that we are actively addressing as an organization."

6. **Context:** Talk about what you care about, why and what you're doing about it. The why is really important. It's important to consider:

- Why is diversity important to you?
- What is your experience with it?
- What is your connection to diversity?

It's important to be cautious in terms of keeping the focus on where it needs to be and not centering on yourself. It helps people understand where you're coming from. It helps them see that your desires are authentic because you can explain where this hope and interest and commitment is coming from.

7. **Geographical considerations:** Your statement should be looking at the issues that are important where you live. I live in British Columbia, Canada, and many of my customers are impacted by different factors based on where they live. Something that's important in my community has been Indigenous issues. My diversity statement talks about my connection to the Indigenous community. I could be talking about the things that I faced and why I, as an Indigenous woman, care about diversity and inclusion.

Another piece to look at is what are the issues that are important where your customers are. Thinking about the issues that are important to your customer is about empathy. Think about what your context is but also think about the context of your customers so that they know you care about what they're experiencing and that there's value alignment.

8. **Authenticity:** Obviously, you want to just include things that you do actually care about because you want to be transparent. You want to be authentic, because people can tell when you're being fake. Even if they can't, having an honest relationship with your audience is important. It's crucial to make sure that your copy reflects your actual position because you want there to be alignment between the words you say and your brand experience.

I've had people come to me and they want me to help them make a statement on an issue because they really care. But if the way they do business isn't aligned with their statement, they're going to spend a lot of money and time attracting people who are ultimately going to be repelled, because the brand experience doesn't reflect their messaging.

9. **Land acknowledgment:** Where does your business operate? Think about which Indigenous territory your business is operating on and include information about that. This is

information you can also include on your contact page where your address goes.

A land acknowledgment is important because people may be interested to know what your relationship is with the local Indigenous community or your position on the issue of returning land to the community. Also, if you are saying that you're operating on the land of a local Indigenous community, look at these related questions:

- How do you steward that land?
- How do you take care of that land?
- How are you sustainable?

The way we take care of the Earth is also inextricably related to whose land it is and how we relate to it. It is not responsible to acknowledge whose territory you're on without actually recognizing the responsibility to take care of that. That's information that you could include in terms of what sustainability and environmental pieces you are pursuing in recognition that you're operating on someone's land.

10. **Positioning:** Another piece to include in your diversity statement is some conversation around what diversity issues your industry faces or perpetuates and how you are oriented towards them. Look at what some of the practices are that you've observed that you've decided not to adopt or that you have phased out or that you plan to phase out. Talk about the issues that are created by your industry and how you deal with them.

With the online coaching industry, this might look like pay equity for offshore contractors. In the wellness industry it might look like ableist fitspiration messaging. Within the diet or fashion industries that might look like patriarchal and racist beauty standards.

11. **Giving credit:** Looking next at issues of cultural appropriation, think about where you have borrowed from culturally to create your product brand or service? This is something you might consider if you are, for example, a white person operating a yoga or belly dancing studio. Or, if you integrate African American music in your workout classes, or if you borrow from other cultures in your recipes in your restaurant.

Consider where your product and service come from and recognize it. Give acknowledgment and props to people that generated this activity, service, product that you love enough to do as your livelihood.

12. **Call to action:** Invite your people along on your journey. Invite them to work with you toward creating more social good. Give them a job, tell them what they can do in order to support your mission. Link the places that you're donating, if you're donating, and link organizations where you're volunteering your time. Invite your people to be part of what you're doing because that's a great way to get them onside. Find a way to include your people.

Next steps: Integration

Now that you have a diversity statement, where does it go? I would suggest creating a standalone page and making it visible immediately when you go on your site. In your top menu make the diversity statement visible and as easy as possible for people to find. If you want to integrate it into an existing page, you might include it on a Values page or your About page.

Digital Blackface: What It Is and How to Avoid It

Teen Vogue did a comprehensive article in August of 2017 called "We Need To Talk About Digital Blackface in Reaction Gifs." Blackface is when you dress up or pretend to be part of a culture to which you don't belong. While it seems innocent on the surface, when you consider the historical context that people have been oppressed for the cultural or racial groups to which they belong, dressing up as a certain person gives you the aesthetic of being part of a community without enduring its hardships. It might even integrate sacred cultural symbolism that might be disrespectful to include and you may not have enough awareness to understand what is sacred and what is a stereotype.

Similarly, in the digital space, the use of memes and gifs that play into stereotypes about groups of people to make a point about how you are feeling reinforces false narratives while providing you with a tool for communication. It's basically using other people's assumptions and often amplifications of ways of being that are stigmatized and leveraging them for your own purposes. It's a little bit making fun of people in a way that makes a point for yourself about your own perspective. It's not respectful and should generally be avoided.

As a best practice, don't use gifs or memes of racialized people that don't represent you. For me, even though I am Indigenous, my skin is very white. I don't feel comfortable using gifs of Indigenous people because people who don't know me won't know that I am part of that group and may think I'm making fun of them. I don't want that. Even though it's the wrong conclusion, it's a distraction from my message. For that reason, I use gifs of Taylor Swift, Kristen Bell, or characters from *Frozen*. These usually express my emotions clearly without me having to adopt the persona of someone who is of a seemingly different race or orientation.

Another way digital blackface can be used is to mimic the speech patterns of another culture to sound cool or trendy. This includes the use of African-American Vernacular English ("sounding Black") to come off edgy. When Black people are socially sanctioned or thought to be less intelligent when speaking this way and face consequences, and you do it to be clever, it can be problematic.

It is only because of your privilege that it is accepted and you are co-opting something that doesn't belong to you when the people who it does belong to can't use it without having issues. This can have a similar effect as a meme or gif that reinforces stereotypes about people who already have challenges navigating the world due to racism. I say racism and not "because of the color of their skin" because the color of their skin is not the problem, it's the attitudes people have about them.

Ultimately, I don't want to communicate in a way that racialized people, or people of a different sexual orientation, or level of ability are stigmatized for as a way to highlight how sassy I am or to amplify and exaggerate my emotions in a relatable way. Borrowing from what might be problematic representation to make a point is irresponsible and I don't know enough to know what is problematic from someone in that community's perspective ... so I think it's easier to default to a more benign way of communicating. This also invites the people who might otherwise be offended by being mocked to listen to your message.

5
YOUR POLICIES:
ARE THEY ABOUT EQUITY?

How to Structure Your Business Policies to Include More People

It is important to have policies in your business because they help your staff make decisions and have standardized ways of dealing with things. If you let people know what they can expect, they can anticipate how they will be accommodated exactly and they know how you plan to treat people. Policies are essentially boundaries that you establish in business much like you establish boundaries in any relationship. Boundaries explain to people what is OK and what is not OK.

One of the frustrations that people have with policy is when they interact with an entity and ask for something that is outside the norm, then they're told that it isn't OK because it's against company policy. In these instances it's valid to consider:

- What is the policy intended to do?

- Why was it implemented?

- What is it designed to protect against?

- Is the exception consistent with the spirit of the policy (if not explicitly described) in it or is it benign in relation to what the policy is trying to stave off?

Policies can create systemic barriers when they are designed by people who don't have an understanding of what other people need or why other people might need different things. They can also be biased when created by people who don't face barriers or who are used to facing barriers that have been normalized.

Policies are basically rules about how people are going to be treated. Accordingly, if you have a value around how people are treated, you need to make sure that your policy reflects those values. It is worth considering having your policies looked at by people from a range of identities so that you can understand how the language and structure of your policies impact people who have less privilege or different life experiences than you.

I talk about inclusion as being more than words but the words that we use in our policy can include or exclude. That is why it's important to think about the language of the policy and whether it reflects the spirit of the policy and whether people look at your policies and see that you value and want to include people. If you don't want to create unnecessary barriers, or you want to eliminate existing barriers, your policies are a great place to start.

Spend time talking to the people impacted by the policies and find out how they feel about them. Get the user's perspective on what that looks like in practice and find out how your staff are interpreting the policy that you have given. It might be that there's a gap between what you intended and what the end users experience, so it's important to be clear and have open dialogue around what the impacts of policies are and how that feels to people on the ground.

Payment Plan Policies

Payment plans is a topic that I learned a lot about from Kelly Diels. Kelly is a consultant in Chilliwack, BC, who writes extensively about the impacts of payment plans on customers. One of the things that I learned is that payment plans — where there is an increased burden for spreading out payments — can sometimes disadvantage people who have been historically excluded over time.

When you charge increased fees to carry a payment plan, people who have less access to capital, credit, or people they can borrow from, end up paying more to work with you than somebody who has not been historically disadvantaged. If you have a value around supporting people from marginalized identities, it's worth looking at whether your payment policy is reflective of that value.

Ultimately, Diels writes, "We've got to apply nuance and analysis, here. Sometimes finance fees are predatory. Sometimes they are not ... I am NOT making a hard policy against mark-ups for payment plans. I'm saying we have to analyze carefully and make justice-informed decisions about our practices." Her essay "Feminist Marketing Tool #626: Reconsider Your Payment Plans because Charging Extra for Payment Plans Can Be Exploitative" has great advice on how to evaluate your payment policies. (www.kellydiels.com/feminist-marketing-tool-626-charging-extra-for-payment-plans-can-be-exploitative, accessed November 2021).

You may not necessarily need to carry the risk of payment plans yourself. There are services such as Sezzle where the business owner is paid up front in exchange for a small fee. The customer deals with Sezzle directly around their payments, and the payments are spread out over a prescribed period of time. I have not used the service as a vendor, but I have as a consumer.

Sometimes the payment processors that we allow people to use can also make a difference in terms of their ability to finance things. If your payment processor doesn't allow for Visa debit cards, you may be disadvantaging and excluding people who historically have struggled with access to credit but would like to buy from you. Similarly, payment gateways such as PayPal can offer financing options to buyers so if you allow people to pay by PayPal, you may be increasing their opportunities to finance their purchases and access what they need.

If someone asks you to accept a method of payment, it's worth looking at whether it makes sense for you and would make it easy for people to pay you and invest in your business. Ultimately, it's your business and how you get paid is up to you but it's worth thinking about whether your payment policies are creating systemic barriers for the very people you say you would like to include.

Another way you can address payments is to make them proportional to the revenue or income of the customer based on a sliding scale. This is a model that business coach and ProfitFirst professional Megan Hale used. "For me, thinking about more equity has really been challenging myself to look at how I can minimize barriers for people who have more obstacles than I do? That can show up with pricing models, like one of my most recent offers had an equitable pricing model. What you paid to be inside this container was based on how much money you are currently making," she explained.

Policies around Accessibility

Accessibility is an important consideration and it's also really key to understand that accessibility isn't just about a wheelchair ramp. It's also about neurodiversity and the way you provide information to your employees or contractors and how you receive work products from them. It's also about the policies that your employees have to navigate and how friendly these policies are to their individual and group circumstances.

I worked with an organization where I was competing for promotions to move up and make more money and because I had a disability, I had to ask for accommodation in the competitive process. Often the tests were handwritten and because of my tremor, I was unable to write by hand for extended periods of time and if I could, the result might be illegible. Because there was no policy to grant an accommodation to an employee and have that accommodation follow them through competitive processes in the future, every time I applied for a job I would have to ask to be accommodated and wait for a response, sometimes delivered within days of the test or interview. There was a lot of uncertainty as to what would be required for proof because there was no standard.

While it was possible to offer the same accommodation to everybody so that nobody had an "advantage" often there were delays which would create stress. My life in trying to get ahead as an employee was more difficult, complicated, and frustrating than that of an able-bodied employee because they didn't have to worry about the same things. They knew that applying for a job would be the same for them every time and that they didn't have to wait for anybody to make decisions around accommodations that would impact their lives.

Another example of accessibility within your business is your policy around punctuality or absenteeism. If you have an attendance management program, have a look at it and see if it is negatively impacting employees who have a disability. You might feel that if in the end they are accommodated, that it is still equitable. If your employees have to jump through a lot of hoops, and go through a lot of frustration, it may be perceived as a barrier and impact their interest in being retained as employees on a long-term basis.

If you are aware that an employee has an issue that might require them to attend more medical appointments, or make their commute more difficult, or have them dealing with variable energy levels, it's worth looking at how this person can be accommodated. People with disabilities still have valuable perspectives that could be informing your work within the organization. Losing out on those perspectives because your policies are not hospitable may disadvantage your company in the long term.

Accommodations that go beyond wheelchair ramps can look like captions on corporate videos; transcripts of corporate training; even live signing and captions during meetings. Working from home can give disabled employees more control over their environment and a better ability to be flexible in managing their health without having to have every piece of their accommodation being approved by human resources.

When you give people the autonomy to manage their wellness and still contribute to work, you are contributing to their self-esteem, their feelings of self-efficacy, and you are showing that their contribution matters, and that you value them enough as humans to believe that they can figure out what it is that they need in order to deliver what it is that you need.

If you have a policy that requires sick notes when people are away, you may be disadvantaging your chronically ill employees. If they have to miss work for being sick, and then they also have to try and get themselves to a medical professional in order to get a sick note and also pay for that sick note, that sick time costs them money.

If you require documentation from a specialist in order to accommodate requests, be aware that sometimes specialists can take months to years to get into, and evaluate how reasonable it is to have that documentation come in that form and whether you can consider trusting your employee to tell you what it is that they need. Specialist reports may also contain information that is deeply personal and that someone shouldn't have to share with their employer. It may not be relevant to the accommodation that they are requesting and some thought should go into how to communicate about somebody's condition in a way that preserves their dignity.That should matter to you as an employer and it's integral to the relationship with your employees that you are respectful and navigate this with them as a partner instead of creating situations that bring undue stress.

If you want to be equitable in your business, the way you treat employees and customers who have disabilities is really important. Take time to educate yourself as to what reasonable accommodations can look like. Have conversations and negotiations with your people so that they get what they need and you get what you need. You can talk about supporting health in the world through your social impact, but the way you deal with actual disabled people within your business is far more telling and provides you with way more opportunities to show that in a meaningful way.

Policies around Wages and Contractor Payments

What and how you pay other people can be indicators of equity. If you aren't paying people a living wage, or if your payment processes are complicated and protracted, you may be attracting less diverse people because the only people who can afford to work with you are people who already have money and are not as concerned about the speed with which they receive their funds.

When I worked in government, we had a payment policy where the processing period was waived in recognition of the fact that Indigenous people often were supporting multiple generations of their families and, in many cases, systemically have less access to capital and credit. Having their checks go through the normal process with a delay would create an inequitable disadvantage for them and serve as a disincentive towards working with the organization.

Is there some way you could be recognizing the circumstances of your staff and your contractors and integrating the realities of their lives into the way that you compensate them? Is there a more reasonable method of payment that you could be implementing? If you're paying by paper checks, is it possible that the banks are holding these checks and creating a delay as to when your employees get access to their funds? Is direct deposit a better option?

When you've dealt with the how, the what you pay is also a really important issue. The issue of what somebody's time is worth is definitely something to spend some time unpacking. Within the online business world there are entire courses that will teach you how to outsource your work to developing nations so that you can pay a lot less with the perception that people living there will be happy with very little money and still have a high standard of living.

The feedback from people who actually live in these countries is that the amount of money that people are being suggested to pay does not necessarily constitute a living wage there either, creating this climate where work from certain countries is not as valuable. This has created situations where contractors will try to implement price increases only to be told that their work is not deserving of more funds because they live somewhere that isn't expensive.

This has been a sticking point in terms of the movement against Asian hate when we might see people speaking out about this issue but at the same time, perhaps refusing to pay a living wage to their Asian contractors. While leveraging optionality in achieving cost savings by minimizing the amount of money you have to spend on labor makes sense, it's important to do that in a way that's ethical and of which you can be proud.

These are some things to think about:

- If one of your offshore team members was speaking to a customer about what their life is like working with your company, how the funds that you pay them contributes to their lifestyle, and their ability to support their family, would you be proud of that?

- Have you taken the time to talk to the people that you have hired and get a sense of what their lives actually look like?

- Have you done recent research into the cost of living in the area where you are spending money? Does the amount you are paying your people still make sense?

- Does it make sense to reward people differently for the value that they are bringing to your business based on where they live and their ethnicity?

- Do your payment structure and business model extract from and exploit people of color or other marginalized groups?

- Does having a regional pay policy align with your values around how you welcome people into your business?

How we pay people and what we pay them matters. The funds that we give to people help them live their lives, maintain their wellness, and afford time to spend with their family pursuing leisure activities and creating that kind of work-life balance that we want to encourage in our employees. You can't have a value of work-life balance but not pay people enough to be able to enjoy that.

When people aren't paid enough in their primary work they have to look for additional employment and that can create negative outcomes and terms of their family, their health, the quality of the work that they do when they show up because of their energy level, and their level of commitment to an organization that hasn't shown commitment to making sure they are OK. What we pay and how we pay people can feel very personal because it impacts their day-to-day lives. These are not just numbers on a spreadsheet, these are choices that have real impacts and it's important to be intentional about what that looks like and to think about how compensation is reflective of your value and who you are as a person and a business owner.

Policies around Charitable Giving

Making charitable giving part of your business is another way you can have a policy of equity. If part of the money that you generate goes towards social causes that are important to you, your business can become a social-impact generating business. We talk a lot about the bottom line but one of the other concepts that is gaining in popularity is the "triple bottom line" and that is a concept that includes profits, people, and the planet.

When you give back through charitable giving you get to use that first "P" of profits and invest in the other Ps: people and the planet. Charitable giving is something that often gets put on the to-do List but without a solid plan to implement it might not happen. Being intentional about your philanthropy is a way to make sure that it actually gets implemented and isn't just a nice idea that you have in your head.

Creating a habit of giving is one of the easier ways to keep going with your charitable giving. Have a process and a plan as to how much you're going to give, when, and where so that making that donation is easy to implement. When you have to think about it and you're not really sure what to do, that's when you could get hung up and not make the donation. When you know exactly how it's going to happen, there are fewer barriers to putting charitable giving into practice in your business.

When you have a defined policy about how much you give, and what kinds of causes you support, you can better explain to people about the social impact your business has. You can talk about it on your website, in all your communications, and with your staff about what the revenue that they're generating goes towards, so they can have a better idea of what they are supporting in the world through their labor. Of course, it isn't just existing staff who are going to want to know about this but also new staff that you might be bringing on board. Tell people about your values and how you stand for them.

This can be a differentiator for you as an employer in a market where getting employees might be more challenging; you can set yourself apart as a company that makes a difference. Many people care about their own triple bottom lines and the way you as a company give back and contribute to their perception of how their energies are being expended will help them envision and contribute to the kinds of change they want to see in the world.

Another way to increase the triple bottom line is to create opportunities for your employees to give. Offer to integrate charitable giving into your payroll systems so that your staff can join together and support causes that matter to them. Talk to your payroll supplier about how you can integrate a company-wide giving policy so that people can voluntarily direct parts of their wages to the causes that matter to them. Of course, make this optional, no pressure: You never know what someone else can afford.

When we talk about charitable giving, it doesn't necessarily have to be cash money that you give, it could be in-kind services or it could be volunteer hours from your executive team or from your staff. You could be donating products or implementing a buy-one-give-one program. One of the more popular examples of this is Toms Shoes: When somebody buys a pair of shoes, Toms donates a pair of shoes to somebody in need. Ruby Cup is a company that does this with menstrual cups for women in developing countries.

There are lots of opportunities to be creative in the way that you give back in the world. Take stock of what you are already doing and what more you would like to do, and develop a plan as to how you're going to transition from your current level of investment to a higher level of investment.

Consider these questions:

- What kinds of things would make you feel more comfortable with giving more?
- What kinds of social issues are important enough to prioritize right now?
- What are the things that your company stands for and what are the charitable organizations that are in alignment with that?
- How can you make best use of the funds that you have available to make the biggest impact in the world?

Charitable giving can be a way of life in your business and with strategic planning and research you can make sure that you can make the most of the resources that you have available and grow your triple bottom line as your business grows.

Giving back is important but your mindset around giving matters too. Megan Hale talked about how she looks at giving and its connection to her overall business. She said, "I think that there's a difference between giving and equitable giving for me. We can give money, but if we don't have other equitable practices that we are integrating into our businesses, giving can be this way where we're trying to wash our hands of something, like, "I donated money. Now I'm good." It's like checking a box. That's not what I really want to create here. I wanted to be giving where we are giving money to equitable organizations, and we're building equitable practices into our businesses."

In her coaching practice, she introduces her clients to what she calls "The 2% Pledge" where they work up to giving 2 percent towards a cause that matters to you. In the broad scheme of things it's a small amount but when companies all over the world give back just a little, it can create a great impact.

Some people get stuck at first because they don't know where to start or where they should give. Hale advises, "The more you give, the more you're going to learn what you're most passionate about giving to, what you most want your money to do, and you'll find more organizations who are connected with that level of work. I think the thing that I want to be a voice for is, we don't need to figure all of that out before we start giving. It's actually in the practice of giving, that we more quickly figure out what type of giving feels best, and what causes matter to us most."

Creating equity in the world can look like giving back but it should also be reflected in the way we do the business that generates those funds. Otherwise, we could be doing harm as we are trying to do good.

Supplier Diversity Policies

When you don't have a big team, one of the ways you can add more diversity to your business is by diversifying your suppliers. Look at all of the pieces of your business and the companies that you involve. Look at all of the supplies that go into the production of your product. Look at all of the software that runs your business. Take some time and do your research and see who owns those companies.

Beyond the demographics of the businesses, do your homework about what kind of social impact these businesses have. Are they giving to causes that you care about? Do they pay their staff to volunteer to support important initiatives? Do they have a diversity statement on their website? What are their values and how do they align with what you believe in?

Ask yourself:

- Would you be proud if somebody knew that you were doing business with these companies? Would you be proud to have your logo on their website?

- When you pay your invoice, are you happy about where the money goes?

- Are there options you can invest in as a customer that you would feel more proud to talk about?

- In doing business with this company, are you missing out on the opportunity to work with somebody who is more aligned?

Take a look at their CEO and what statements they have publicly made on social issues. Look at the way they run their business and how they value their staff. Spend some time on their social media and Google them to see what kind of news mentions come up.

If you find that your current suppliers are not aligned with your values, and there are things that could change, consider having that conversation with them. Let them know that you're taking stock of your partnerships and looking for alignment, and identify the areas where you have concerns. Ask them to take a look at those issues and see if they're receptive to feedback.

If they are receptive and open to changing, then that might be a partnership that is worth continuing. But just like Sonya Perkins of Forever Yours Lingerie found back in Chapter 1, money talks and if they are continuing to be out of alignment with you, but it's important to you, it's fair to find a supplier that is more aligned with your values. Giving people an opportunity to surprise you and improve their business is a respectful way to interact, but be aware that just like you run your business a certain way for your own reasons, they may not be open to change at this time. That's OK too, but you don't have to stay working with them if it doesn't feel right to you anymore.

Now that you've taken stock of the level of diversity within your suppliers, you can take a look at what other options are available in the market and if there is a way that you can be supporting businesses that are owned by people who are members of historically excluded groups. Take a look at what other solutions are available on the market and whether working with them would help improve the diversity within your business.

You don't have to have a big team in order to bring more diversity into your business. You can collaborate with other business owners and invest in businesses that are aligned with your worldview. Your suppliers are essentially collaborators in your business, so it's important to think about how the people you work with reflect your values and make some changes, if needed.

6

MARKETING TO AND FOR MORE PEOPLE

Marketing is the way you position yourself in front of your audience to make sales and generate brand awareness. It's how you talk about what you do, who you are, who you serve, what makes you different (your unique value proposition), and the choices you make that help you make a good first or ongoing impression to your audience.

Whether you choose to advertise online, with flyers, direct mail, display advertising, or any number of other methods, your messaging needs to be strong and impactful to mitigate the dwindling attention spans of the general public. Ideally, you want to be remembered for good reasons.

Inclusive Content

Inclusive content is messaging and imagery that resonates with a range of people, delivered in a format they can access.

What does inclusive content feel like? When people can see themselves in a relationship with your brand, they feel like their lives, values, and struggles are understood, and they feel like representations of them are respectful and accurate, your content feels inclusive.

Even with the right intentions, a marketing message can fall flat. For International Women's Day, Burger King tweeted, "Women belong in the kitchen." It was an opening line for a message about scholarship programs the company would be offering, but the follow-up message was delayed and there was a lot of time where people who genuinely agreed with the tweet had a field day in the comments. People were pretty mad. Fingers were pointed. Keyboards lit up screens with opinions.

It was successful in being memorable but not necessarily in garnering the goodwill of the public. A similar ad appeared in print and it was on other social media platforms. What wasn't lost on commenters was that the brand spent more money advertising its program than it actually offered in the program. This earned them some snark about the messaging being performative. Someone suggested the company could have won the internet with a tweet that simply said "Burger Queen."

Ultimately, there were many ways the program and the way it was shared could have been designed better and been more aligned with the brand's goal to support the aspirations of women. It was a shame, because earlier campaigns to encourage ordering food from restaurants over the COVID-19 pandemic were very much "collaboration over competition" and had a "feel good, do good" flavor to them.

Similarly, over the pandemic, brands created a whole genre of ads that spoke the need to come together apart, to support public health, to thank healthcare staff, and to provide a sentiment that the brands cared about customers. While the similarity in language among ads was widely panned and were felt to be a bit "cringey" at times, it represented unity in messaging focused on a common goal of community wellness, even from brands not normally associated with wellness.

Ultimately, you can market to bring in more people or you can market to bring in a broader range of people and those aren't necessarily the same thing. Inclusive marketing is a form of marketing that shares the values of the business owner and shares a message that the brand is intentional about the way it includes people.

Without specific details, if the messaging organizations aren't careful, these campaigns can be seen to be performative, aspirational, and lacking in substance. They are sometimes cynically viewed as puff pieces designed to ingratiate a brand to an audience who cares about these things without actually doing anything meaningful or making any commitments around what that looks like.

Inclusive marketing doesn't have to be performative; there are ways advertising and messaging can be impactful, inspiring, and informative. You just need to think it through and keep some things in mind.

If you're planning on integrating a social justice value in your campaign, it's a good idea to be specific. If you as a brand are doing something definitive around a social issue, talk about what that is. If you are making strides to make your menu more allergy-friendly to welcome more people into your restaurant, talk about that, for example.

Don't just talk about it, be about it

"We believe everyone should have access to delicious, high-quality food," is a lot less informative and specific than, "We see you, parents of kids with allergies. You want your family to enjoy mouthwatering meals without having to worry about The Big 8 allergens. That's why we've made a shift ... because we believe everyone should have access to delicious, high-quality food, even if they have reactions to the most common allergens. We've done X, Y, and Z to keep our most vulnerable diners safe from all the discomfort that comes from ingesting something your body just can't process without setting off a histamine reaction. Join us for dinner so you can eat a little healthier and breathe a little easier. If you've got food allergies, we've got you."

You move from performative to transformative when you take action and document it. Your advertisements could be artistic forms of brand journalism, not just brand broadcasts. When you move from feeling to doing, that's where the magic happens and people believe you mean what you say. You can point to something that serves as evidence that this isn't just a feel-good, performative thing.

Giving together is better

Apart from process improvements that fill a need for justice that your customers are facing, you could also enlist your customers in philanthropy. You can give a corporate donation to a cause you believe in but when you involve your audience as coconspirators for good, you get to give back and your audience has the experience of being a part of something.

You can use social media, your brick-and-mortar location, and your email marketing as a way to mobilize your audience for good. If you let your audience be a part of the solution, you can create change in the world together. Being seen as a connection point and as community-driven can only be a good thing.

If you are planning to pledge a portion of your revenue for a cause in a given month, that's another way to get people involved. They know that the money they were planning on spending anyway is going to a cause they believe in and it might get them motivated to add a little something extra to their shopping cart, increasing the impact of your giving intention.

Have a goal

Outside of brand awareness and driving sales, what social impact do you want your ad to have? These are some helpful questions to ask yourself along the way as you map where you want your campaign to go:

- What are you hoping will come of it?
- Are you hoping to reflect the diversity you see in the world?
- Are you looking to increase equity in the world through a specific action?
- Are you looking to celebrate a portion of your audience that are historically excluded?
- Are you hoping to make your position known on an important social issue?
- Are you wanting to communicate a policy, process, or product change that will have a social impact?
- Are you announcing an initiative that will make a difference?

If you keep your eye on the prize, you're more likely to win the hearts and minds of your followers and fans. If you don't have a goal for your campaign, you won't be able to measure the extent to which it met the requirements and achieved what it needed to achieve.

Keep It Simple

Keep your message clear and consistent. Make it easy for people to join in. Help your audience understand how the cause you are supporting is connected to you and your brand so they don't have to think about it too much. Be clear about the intended action, the potential impact, what their role is, and what yours is.

Your marketing can have a tangible impact, reflect your brand values, raise awareness of your brand, drive sales, and increase the connection and affinity to your brand all at the same time. Doing the right thing doesn't have to be exclusive of generating revenue, you can drive profits and impact simultaneously, but you just need to approach it with class and with clear intentions, and help your audience understand how things can change.

Representation

I remember the first time I saw an Indigenous Santa Claus. Growing up all the Santas were old white men and I had never seen a Santa that looked like me or like men from my community. Then one day I opened a newsletter and saw an Indigenous Santa Claus. My heart leapt. It felt so good to feel seen and felt and to have a different kind of connection to the character of Santa Claus that reflected my identity and values.

Representation can be powerful and can evoke a strong emotional response in the viewer. One of the ways marketing can be inclusive is by increasing representation. The repetition of ad touch points also serves to reinforce and celebrate people from historically excluded groups just by virtue of the frequency of exposure that makes ads effective. But how does it work?

There are a few layers in terms of how representation in marketing can have an impact. It's important to be clear what your goal is in terms of creating representation.

Representation in media

One goal for creating representative advertising is that you are creating content that helps people see themselves represented in media. You want to create a moment where people feel seen and represented on screen, in stories, in imagery; it can be artistic, aspirational, and fill gaps in representation that you've seen in advertising.

Representation in relation to your brand

Outside of helping people see themselves in advertising generally, you might also be trying to relay the idea that people who belong to a specific group can be well served by your brand and are welcome. For your audience, it says, "You can find people like you here."

Unfortunately, that only really works if you can. If you are using advertising to create a false picture of the diversity in your business without first readying your space, addressing barriers to service, or ensuring you are actually able to provide culturally responsive products or services that will meet the needs of the audience you are appealing to, that's premature.

Another challenge comes when it's a one-off initiative and there's no attempt to keep that representation going. When you look back on the Instagram feed you see there was that one week where there were a lot of diverse people and the feed was a bit more colorful, but then it went back to mostly white people, it looks like the people of color were a blip. Being intentional about ongoing representation is important to demonstrate that you have an ongoing commitment.

Something to keep in mind is that it's only helpful to show representation of people you are actually equipped to serve. If you are a hairstylist but don't have experience doing Black hair, you're going to want to make sure your content reflects your skillset. Similarly, if your restaurant is at the top of a second-storey walkup, it doesn't make sense to show wheelchair users who will not be able to access your space.

You also need to make sure that the representation you use is not perpetuating negative stereotypes. If you want to celebrate Asian culture, using stock images of tourists with cameras is probably not the way to go. Be aware that people from many groups have been portrayed one-dimensionally. If you want people to feel seen, heard, and felt, using the same old tired images and words they have been sick of for years isn't going to win points or have the desired effect.

Not all representation is good. Think about "cowboys and Indians" in old Western movies. That's not a positive example of representation. A better example of representation is something like *Rutherford Falls*, which is a sitcom about Indigenous people written by Indigenous people, so it's relatable and not dehumanizing. Being ethical about your representation is important because it's not about just making your feed more colorful, it's about respecting people in your content and showing you respect them.

Simply put, representation is powerful if it's reflective, realistic, and reinforced through ongoing repetition. Be clear about why you want to use representation in your content and be thoughtful about how you do it. A picture is worth a thousand words, but you need to be aligned with the message it sends for it to be effective.

An alternative way you can get diverse images is through influencer content. If you engage influencers from different communities, that can be a good way to get some more representation. If you're going to engage an influencer, it's really important to be clear about the rights you are requesting and the intended use of the images.

If you are going to commission some content, make sure that your agreement fully explains all of the places and ways that you want to be able to use the content that they produce, because that may (fairly) impact any pricing they may set. Set yourself up for success with your influencer relationships by being really clear about your intentions. A miscommunication can impact your relationship with the community they belong to if somebody that's respected within that community has had a negative experience with your brand.

Create a Cohesive Brand Experience

It's one thing to say the right thing but if it isn't true, then it isn't helpful. If you go out of your way to design a campaign around a value, it's important to be sure that that value is part of the brand experience. If you say that you are a brand that is about accepting all bodies, but when people come into your gym they encounter fatphobia and diet culture messaging then they aren't going to stick around. They are going to walk out the door because they've been let down and sold a bill of goods that wasn't reflective of the merchandise. They came in order to have an experience with a brand that was body positive and if they find the opposite when they arrive, it isn't going to be an ongoing relationship because you haven't followed through on the brand promise you made in your advertising.

What it means to have cohesive brand experience: The message needs to match the experience andboth of those match the values so it all hangs together effectively. When you create messaging that isn't in alignment with what you believe, or with what people will actually experience in the context of your brand, you're going to lose people. You're also going to look inauthentic and there's going to be an erosion of trust.

Often, I am approached about how to say the right thing but if you aren't doing the right thing then saying the right thing isn't going to help. When you're consistent in what you say and what you do it helps build trust with your clients. People know what to expect and they know that when you say something that you mean it.

It is important to get clear on what your values are and beyond that how someone could tell what your values are in the experience of doing business with you. How do people know that you believe what you believe? If you have a value and you share about it in your marketing, is it reflected in the policies, procedures, and the day-to-day culture of your business?

Values don't only impact your customer retention or churn rate, they are also something that will impact your ability to recruit and retain employees. If you recruit employees to join a mission that they are aligned with and when they arrive their role is the exact opposite, they are not going to want to stay. They are also not going to trust that you're going to do what you say you're going to do because you told them you were going to do something and you did the opposite.

For employees who are driven by their values this can feel like a betrayal. It can leave people with a bad feeling about your brand and it can create frustration and disillusionment. If someone left meaningful work to work that with you, and it turns out that the work doesn't actually align with their values, they might feel resentful that they gave up another opportunity thinking that they would be able to work in a way that they were comfortable.

Creating a cohesive brand experience involves ensuring that your external and internal communication is consistent with the brand experience that people have whether customer, employee, or supplier. When you do this, people know what you're about and what they can count on from you. When your brand experience and your brand message are in alignment then people can vote with their dollars for the things they believe in and know that their vote has been counted.

It isn't enough to fix the message if you haven't fixed the inner workings of the business. Sometimes, when you fix the inner workings of your business, the way you talk about what you do changes too. It can be a bit of a chicken-and-egg scenario, but ultimately both things need to be present. You need a clear authentic message, and you need accurate and corresponding implementation.

Equitable Advertising Tactics

If you're looking to be more equitable in your advertising, it's important to think about what strategies you're using. There are some questions you need to ask yourself:

- Where are you placing ads?

- Are you positioning your ads so that people who are different than your normal audience will see them?

- When you think about the ad content that you are targeting towards the people that you're looking to attract, is it content that will resonate with them?

If you want to expand access to your offering, you need to be able to promote effectively using language and imagery that is familiar to your intended audience, in the places where they normally spend time. It isn't helpful to keep advertising in the same places, hoping for a different result and to keep using the same messaging that consistently hasn't attracted the kinds of people you're looking to include. You have to consider that how, where, and when a new audience consumes content may be different based on their lifestyle.

You might need to have a different plan in order to reach different people. Part of that comes down to what they value or how they talk about what they value, or whether they can relate to the scenarios that you put in your ad.

You need a well-placed message that resonates in order to expand your access to a broader audience. If you're looking to attract certain groups of people, it might be helpful to focus test your advertising with members of that group to see how it lands and what potential challenges might exist with your concept.

Equitable advertising also considers the socioeconomic context and the social history of the audience. An example of an inequitable or unethical marketing tactic might look like something you are used to seeing day in and day out: before and after pictures for weight loss. In these situations, a certain body ideal is being put forward as the most desirable.

The reason this is problematic is that fatphobia is often rooted in white supremacy, because the beauty ideal being presented is typically one of whiteness. Even the body mass index (BMI) was developed based on white people and did not include culturally diverse bodies. The standards that the BMI's norm of what is "healthy" are inherently racist and exclude the experiences of people of color.

Another way advertising can be inequitable is when a testimonial is presented as if anybody could achieve a similar result without considering factors such as race and proximity to wealth which can also be influenced by race and available resources with which to take risks. You also have to look at access to capital, and any systemic barriers people face based on race or other personal factors. That's why it's not as cut-and-dry as to say "if you follow this method you will see certain results." The reality may be quite different for somebody with fewer resources, who belongs to a community that has not historically had their work devalued.

One way white supremacist myths are perpetuated in online business advertising is in the advertisement of courses that teach you how to outsource the work that you need done overseas. These courses present a false narrative that you can pay people of a certain race or ethnicity a very small amount and that there is no harm associated with doing so.

The idea that someone's work is less valuable because of where they live or what their ethnicity is can be incredibly damaging. It sends a message to the audience who may be a member of that group that their work is not valuable or that you don't think that they should be well paid for their services.

Being equitable and ethical in your advertising is about what you say, where are you saying, how you say it, and how it reflects the relationship that you want to have with your audience. This is part of having consistency within your brand. If you say you care about people, then also you should pay them well. It's easy to care about theoretical people you may never meet but it's a whole other thing to intentionally build your business around welcoming people who are different from you and making sure that the advertising you do is not harmful.

7
BUILDING INCLUSIVE COMMUNITIES ONLINE

When we talk about online communities, we might initially think about Facebook groups or membership communities. The term "online community" can equally apply to groups interacting in or with on social media channels, newsletters/email marketing, and any way that we interact online where people are assembled based on an affinity or interest in a topic, perspective, or product.

Your inclusive online community might be the means to advertise your product or service, or it may be how you actually deliver those products or services. How you show up online impacts how people see your business. How you conduct yourself online might be the only interaction people get with you, depending on your business. It is often the first impression but it might be the only impression you get. This is why, if inclusion is something you value, building an inclusive online community is important.

How to Build a Diverse and Inclusive Online Community

Building an inclusive online community is about both recruitment and retention. Recruitment is about how you call people into your community. Here are some questions to ask yourself if you find your community isn't that diverse:

- Do you have an opt-in piece, content, or freemium (valuable freebie) that solves problems for people from a variety of experiences and backgrounds?

- Is your opt-in or content appealing to people who are different from you?

- Where are you advertising? Are you advertising in places where people who are different from you will have access to the information?

- Do you have relationships with influencers from the communities you hope to attract?

- Have you made it evident the space you're inviting them to is anti-oppressive/welcoming?

- Is your language inclusive?

- Have you considered a (paid!) focus group with the kinds of people you are looking to attract to get their opinions on why you aren't getting people joining or where there might be a disconnect?

- Do you have the skills, experience, facilities, and infrastructure to serve the people you are wishing you could welcome?

When you're thinking about what people will experience once recruited to your community, these are some questions to ask yourself:

- Are there other people who share their experiences, perspectives, or worldview?

- Does the space focus on experiences they can't relate to, leaving them feeling left out?

- Does the culture of the group value the contributions of a variety of perspectives?

- How do you foster a sense of belonging across a variety of demographics?

- Does the information or experience in the community add value to people who are not like you?

- Are there barriers to accessing or enjoying the community for people not like you that you might not have experienced?

The thing is, if you welcome people into a space that isn't ready for them, you're going to have a higher rate of attrition. If you welcome people into a space that isn't welcoming on the inside, full of people not ready to receive them, staffed with team members who don't understand what they need or what barriers might exist for them, they may not stick around.

When people leave because the space isn't ready, you've invested a lot of money, time, or energy in calling people you weren't prepared to keep. That's an expensive proposition and you could be perpetuating harm in the process. It's not just that you're losing money, it's that people could be getting hurt or not served adequately in the process.

When you have a bunch of people who are having a negative experience, that can get around and make diversifying your community even harder because word has spread. This is why being intentional and thoughtful about your approach to recruit and retain new community members is important.

Being ready before you welcome people is long-term reputation management; it protects your brand, it creates positive brand experiences, and offers brand journalism opportunities you can leverage based on the success of your members.

If you find you're losing a large number of members, and it is skewing toward attrition of specific groups of people, it's worth looking at whether an exit interview can point to the retention issues that need to be addressed. It's helpful to incentivize people to participate to show that you value their time. If it's intel that's going to benefit your business, it's helpful to pay people as consultants to point you in the right direction.

Another thing to look at is the concept of creating a safe space versus a brave space. This is a practice that I heard advocated for by Megan Hale, an entrepreneur who was interviewed for and who is mentioned throughout this book. The premise is that there is acknowledgment that there is harm, but that there is intention around how people interact, the culture of the group, an awareness that we can do hard things, that we see inclusion as a practice, and that it is a practice that is ever-evolving. We can't promise that nobody will feel challenged, but we can let people know what to expect and do our best to be equitable and ethical in how we operate.

Online Community Conflict Resolution

Conflict that happens online can escalate quickly. It can spread fast and far in a blink of an eye and that kind of momentum can be scary as a business owner. There are ways to reduce the risk of online conflict and also ways to minimize the impact by being proactive and intentional about how you set up your community.

Team up against trauma

First, you're going to want to, as best you can, implement a diverse moderation team if your budget allows. If you can't hire multiple people, ensuring the person who is managing your community has appropriate training is a good best practice.

A diverse moderation team is going to be more likely to spot subtle acts of exclusion (or what are more commonly known as microaggressions) because they have been in situations where they have encountered that behavior before. Being trained in how to address and diffuse those situations is also important. It isn't just outright hate speech that makes people feel unwelcome, it can also be a culture where exclusion continues unchecked that can cause uncomfortable feelings of oppression.

Don't "dirty delete"

Consider the silent readers and don't delete instances of conflict or interactions where learning happened. If you delete it, there's been a lot of strife, maybe the people involved learned something, but nobody else will have the opportunity to learn. Dealing with conflict and leaving evidence that you handle situations as they arise will help people know the space is moderated.

When people who have been historically excluded (or anyone) take the time to educate other people about why behavior isn't OK, they are expending emotional labor. It can be an emotionally charged thing to stand up and say, "This isn't OK. This is why. This is my experience." When you erase comments, you devalue the emotional labor that went into that expression. It can leave people questioning the value assigned to their contributions and whether their presence adds value. They might feel like they don't belong or like they aren't appreciated. When you erase something that happens within your community, you have a larger chance of those grievances being aired publicly elsewhere because people don't feel heard.

For communities where harm against them has been swept under the rug for years, decades and centuries, erasing their feedback and words can feel like just another incursion. The response you receive is likely to be a triggering of the cumulative erasure some populations may have experienced, and may seem disproportionate to the simple act of deleting something.

Set boundaries like a boss

Let people know ahead of time what's OK in your space so they know how to behave. They may still make other choices you don't appreciate, but at least let them know what the standards are. Teach people how to treat you and be up front about what it is you want to see happening in your community. Post your rules around expected behaviors of contributing community members.

When you're developing your rules, think about whether they are equitable. They might not be a problem for you, but what about people who don't have your privilege? Are you asking too much? Are you asking too little? Think about how your rules impact people and what you want to see happen by having a rule.

When it comes to enforcing boundaries, it might be helpful to be brief. The longer, the more meandering your response can be, the more reasons someone might find to challenge it. It doesn't need to be an essay response. You can simply say, "This is not consistent with our community agreement. Please refer to the parameters of our community agreement for more information about how we relate to each other here." Or simply, "We don't do that here. Let's try something else in the future because that wasn't a productive way for us to interact." It can be uncomfortable at first, especially if you're not feeling super confident, but in time it will become something you're used to.

Setting boundaries as a business owner is something you likely already know how to do, it might just be new in this context or subject matter area. We set boundaries as business owners all the time in terms of payment, around when something's going to be completed, around how much we're going to do, how fast, how long, how many times, these are all ways we set boundaries all the time.

It's important to be mindful in boundary enforcement the social history of the people you are speaking with and who are watching the boundary enforcement. People from historically excluded communities have experiences with disproportionate enforcement of the rules and so this can be a sensitive topic when there's a sense of injustice and a legacy of feeling like restrictions are unevenly applied.

Forbidden topics

Decide early on what topics are off limits within the group. How do people know what they are? How do you handle situations when these topics come up? This is really important to decide in advance. There are some topics that will create more conflict than others. It's important to decide whether you have a specific position on it as a group, whether it's something you're open to having debated, and what is going to help people stay on topic and focused on what they need to do within your group. Being front about it can eliminate arguments, confusion, and upsets later.

Tone policing

When rules are made around communication expectations, consider the impact of tone policing. Are you expecting marginalized people to respond gracefully to potentially dehumanizing experiences? Is that a reasonable expectation? Are you trying to reduce conflict or are you hoping for a just outcome (because those aren't always the same thing!)?

It can be really challenging for somebody who has come from a marginalized community who's experienced something, to have people who have never experienced that and never will, tell them how they should feel about it and how they should talk about it. Help your group understand what tone policing is, how it's expected to be handled in your group, and what the guidelines are around language.

Content warnings

A content warning or a trigger warning is a way to give people a heads-up about what they are going to be encountering so they can decide whether or not they want to interact with a piece of content. Determine what gets a content warning and to be clear about how you do one properly.

If you want to use a content warning, it's usually good to write "content warning" and information about what the nature of the content is and then to create enough space between the content warning to hide the content below the fold, so that the person who's encountering the post can make a decision about whether or not they want to interact with content.

Someone posting something with a content warning might be concerned about the images (and might limit them to being in the comments versus as part of the post itself), or discussions around sensitive topics that might be upsetting or triggering. It's something that can make sense if you're wanting to keep people focused on learning. It's not helpful for people to be upset by things unrelated to the experience and why they are there.

Obviously, you don't want to traumatize people. It's impossible to predict what is going to trigger somebody but there are some topics you can logically predict that people are going to feel upset about, such as the loss of a child. If you're in an eating disorder group, maybe discussions around weight loss could be problematic. Having a process to manage difficult conversations can make people more likely to feel comfortable in your inclusive online community.

Dealing with exclusion

Another policy is needed around microaggressions or "subtle acts of exclusion." Sometimes that expression is preferred because microaggressions can give the impression that it isn't really a big deal when it's an unintended statement or action that can leave people feeling uncomfortable.

A microaggression can be the impact of a connotation of a word or the history of an expression, or a compliment that comes out wrong and has the opposite effect. A common example is when a person of color speaks on something, produces something, does something, and somebody says, "Wow, they're so articulate." It's almost like saying, "I didn't expect you to be this smart."

That's not what's intended, but because there has been so much bias around people being perceived to be "less than," an expression that indicates surprise or that it's unexpected that somebody might have a level of competency, can feel uncomfortable.

Knowing how to deal with those in the moment, and how to empower your members to have courageous conversations is important. To be able to say, "Hey, I know you meant that as a compliment and I love that you're impressed by my work. But when I hear you say, X, Y, or Z, this is how I'm feeling. I would love to be honored this way. For me being honored for my talents might sound like this ... "

This kind of guided conversation helps people understand how they can honor each other and how to call out statements that indicate bias so they can have frank conversations about them. Being OK with the discomfort and learning how to manage it as a community is key.

Outrage porn

Outrage porn is content intended to upset people. It doesn't have a goal, there's no action from it; you post it and you're mad, and you want other people to be mad, too. It doesn't do anything except upset everybody. It's good to have policies and limits around what kinds of content can be posted, and to develop a community consciousness around reflecting on how people are going to be impacted by your posts.

You might ask yourself: What is the point of posting it? Is it upsetting people for no reason? Is there a goal? Is there a call to action? Can people do something about it? Or is this just about being mad and creating a space where people are angry? It's important to be aware, to witness injustice, know that it's happening, and be able to name and call it out. But it's important to do that in a productive way that doesn't create more trauma.

Angry spaces can be unproductive, inhospitable, and make people too uncomfortable to share as they learn. When people know other people in the group have a culture of being incendiary, putting oneself out there can be even more intimidating. That isn't what you want in a group that is inclusive, where people who are loudest have the power to silence people with their propensity for outrage.

Managing the flow

In order to address issues such as content warnings and outrage porn, you might look at posting boundaries within your Facebook group and whether posts need to be moderated before they're posted. Consider whether new members need a period of time to acclimatize themselves before they're permitted to post. Does it make sense, when you have new intakes to the group to pause posts for a period of time for people to get a feel for the culture?

Communities of purpose (and permanence)

You need a purpose for your community. If your community doesn't have a job, or a goal, it can become stagnant and people can get into unproductive debate and drama. That's why it's really important to have a focus for your group and for people to have a reason to be there and things to do. '

It's important to look at the intake cycle. Are you letting in people in waves so that they can learn together? Are you bringing in people one at a time where people are always individually learning the culture of the group? What is going to be best for the balance of your group?

Something else to look at is the permanence of your group. Is it intended to be a long-term community? Or is it a pop-up? You may need to be more intentional with a longer term group in order to keep things moving, to keep the conversations and the work happening, productive, and focused. You should also look at what activities create group cohesion and community.

Some other considerations:

- What are the things that people in your community do together?
- What is their identity as group members?
- What feeds their sense of belonging?
- What helps them feel significant to the group?
- How do people belong to each other and to the group and to you?
- How do people relate and stick together?
- What are the things that the group is built on?
- How do you bring people back to the purpose and inspire them to focus?

I have learned from a great many people in the process of developing these guidelines and areas for reflection. The concept of outrage porn is something that I learned from the moderators of a group called Eating The Food. They also taught me about the concept of antifragility and the moderation best practices they used have informed my perspectives on group moderation and community building.

Justice versus peace

Obviously we want people to have fun in our communities and enjoy themselves. But if conflict reduction comes at the cost of justice and people feeling seen, heard, and felt, is it still fulfilling your mandate of creating a space where people enjoy themselves? Or is it creating a space where only certain people enjoy themselves? Are you OK with that?

It might be you've made a judgment call that you are OK with those people who show up and spew hate speech being uncomfortable. You might have made a decision that you're OK with people out of alignment with your brand messaging not being comfortable if their opposite position interferes with your business operations or reduces the effectiveness of your messaging.

Whatever you decide, be intentional about it and be clear about if the approach you're taking reflects your values and how you want to be known in the world. Thinking about family dynamics, families where nobody ever fights aren't always the happiest, they can be full of pent-up resentment, passive aggression, and lack a sense of meaningful belonging.

Finding middle ground and nuance between a conflict-free zone and complete anarchy is a necessary practice. Leaving room for expression while not tolerating hate speech is a line that has to be walked. It will take time to find the balance, but it's worth looking for and striving toward.

Setting expectations around privacy

Privacy is something that you're going to want to have in your inclusive community depending on the venue and the parameters. You need to be clear; are screenshots allowed in your group? What information needs to be confidential? You need for your group members to understand how people are impacted by breaches.

The reality is that there may be additional safety considerations for marginalized people in your group that need to be considered when it comes to privacy. That's why it's really important to be clear about what the privacy expectations are. Ultimately, people are going to do what they're going to do and you can't control that, but you can be clear about your expectations.

What Happens If I Screw up? (Letting Go of Moral Perfectionism)

The reality is that because you're human, more than likely you will screw up. It's really more of a question about what you do in response to a mistake that really matters. How do you handle it? How do you get back into the right relationship with your audience? How do you repair harm? When you have a relationship with your audience, and you're interacting as humans, there are bound to be misunderstandings. Being able to handle them with grace is the goal, along with being able to prevent them as much as possible.

When you mess up, that is the time to flex your compassion muscles. Be compassionate towards the people who have been impacted by the choices that you've made and also toward yourself, because if you get stuck in a reactive, shameful space, you're not going to be able to make the best decisions. The parts of your brain that help with decision making just aren't accessible when you're in an elevated state.

Taking some time to be compassionate, and to calm yourself down will help you make better choices in the moment. Once you're able to think things through, reflect on what went wrong. How did we get here? What happened? Where was the communication breakdown? Problem-solve from there.

Megan Hale talked about how she's navigated moral perfectionism in her journey, explaining, "I've had to realize that it's a moment-to-moment practice of being racist or antiracist. You're never going to get to a point, I don't think, where you'll never have to practice your tools or do your own inner work around it. And so for white people in particular, I think being called a racist can feel like the most scary thing ever. It's this repulsive term. I think something powerful happens when you discharge that word.

"We attach these binaries to it. That if you're racist, you must be a horrible person. And surely, there are horrible racists. But what I think is far more important to realize is that we can hold many loving, kind, generous characteristics and still be racist. Dissolving the binary has been everything!

"And so, there are racist beliefs ingrained in me that I continue to dismantle over and over and over again, and I don't know how long I'll be doing it until the work is done. Maybe it's never done. But I think owning that about yourself is something that can help depersonalize it a little bit. Because we're all swimming in the same water; we're all breathing the same air. Every single person on this planet has work to do around that of unlearning, dismantling, and unplugging from those systems, white people just likely have more."

We are never going to be perfect, but that doesn't mean we shouldn't still try our best. So often, people say, "these are difficult conversations" in relation to talking about social issues. That expectation that they are difficult seems to absolve them of the responsibility to be prepared and do their homework. The idea that it will be messy no matter what so show up and see what happens isn't reflective of a growth mindset. It doesn't have to be an all-or-nothing thing.

You can know that the conversation is going to be difficult and be as prepared as possible and show up educated to talk about it. You can reduce the amount of harm that can come from a conversation by taking the time to research and get ready. Coming with the attitude, "I can't possibly know how to respond perfectly no matter how much I prepare so I may as well wing it," isn't a response that puts value on the relationship. When you care about someone, you think about what matters to them and how you can relate to them better. You might not always get it right, but you can try.

Moral perfectionism is a tricky thing. When we get fixated on doing everything perfectly, we leave the door open to a shame spiral when we screw up. It's not about doing things perfectly, it's about doing things better and trying. Imperfect movement forward that results in more inclusion is inherently an improvement. If you wait until you have the time, energy, and funds to implement a perfect plan, you miss out on incremental improvement that comes from letting go of moral perfectionism.

The other thing that happens when you adhere to moral perfectionism is that it shapes your interactions with others. Being too rigid in your expectations doesn't leave room for people to be humans having human experiences and learning from mistakes. When you have a good or bad binary, you don't have space for nuance, the quality of conversations you can have degrades and there's a sense of scarcity around your interactions. You lose the opportunity to appreciate the good and better because you're stuck on doing it right.

There are best practices and there are norms to be aware of but there isn't always a perfect way to do something. If you wait to find the perfect answer, you may never get started. Committing to educating yourself so you can start moving forward is the best plan. Moral perfectionism isn't helpful and it makes it so much harder to recover when you fail (and makes "failure" immensely more likely).

Diversity, equity, and inclusion is a practice. It's something we pursue and work towards every day. Just like any discipline, the norms and best practices will shift over time. Languages are living and preferred words to describe things may shift with time and discourse.

This can lead to a sense of frustration, "What will they want next?," "I can't keep up with all of this PC stuff," "It never used to be like this," etc., but the reality is that every field evolves, every facet of a business is subject to modernization, so why should talking to our customers be any different?

The less you look at it as a hostage negotiation and the more you look at it as a means of constant quality improvement, the easier it will be to navigate. When you accommodate out of obligation and come at these things with a sense of resentment or woundedness, it doesn't come across in a welcoming way.

Ultimately, being inclusive is about welcoming more people. When you pursue a relationship with your audience, when you approach communications as an opportunity for dialogue versus broadcast, things can come up, just like in any relationship. But being tuned in with your people, having empathy, and approaching conflict thoughtfully can go a long way.

The Anatomy of an Apology

When it comes time to apologize, it's important to be intentional about how you make things right with your audience. There are things that should be in an apology and some things that should not. Many times, situations could be resolved with a simple apology, but doing it wrong can create even more outrage.

This is something that was seen in the online business world when posts and comments were being deleted or disallowed about social issues in 2020 in Facebook groups associated with business coaching programs or communities. When there was outcry from membership, people leading the community delivered apologies that weren't well received. There were tears, blameshifting, qualified apologies, or non-apologies.

The impact was a lot of repair needed in the relationships, an erosion of trust and reputation, and a degradation of the brands. Some audience members left as a result. In one case, the business owner stepped down from the management of their own group and the people calling them out went viral. It would have been something very distressing for a business owner to experience and it was hard to watch, frankly.

The way you handle adversity illuminates your values and can say a lot about who you are as a person. The reality is that in these situations, it's understandable to feel defensive and overwhelmed. It can get emotional and there's a pressure to respond in the moment. That can lead to impulsive responses and you may not have time to regulate yourself emotionally.

Feedback can feel intensely personal, especially if you have a personality-driven brand that focuses on you as the business owner. It might be advisable to connect with a therapist to de-escalate and get yourself situated for the most effective response.

Here's what not to put in an apology:

1. **Blame:** When you shift the blame to someone else, the sincerity of your apology gets called into question. What are you apologizing for if it's not your fault? Even if it was someone on your team, take the "L" as the leader. You can explain how it happened, but be aware of the optics of publicly throwing your team under the bus.

   Explanations are fine, excuses are less fine. Taking radical responsibility is something your people will appreciate. Something else that is not an apology is, "I'm sorry you were upset by this." That isn't taking responsibility, that's focusing the communication on the reaction instead of the action that led you to this place.

2. **Tears:** If you've done harm, centering yourself by focusing on your reaction to the accountability you're facing isn't going to land well. Keep the focus on the people who have been harmed and don't make it about you. What happens when you get overly emotional in an apology is that the onus on taking care of you goes to the listener or the person receiving the apology, and there is a sense of obligation to take on emotional labor to comfort you. Don't give people you've hurt responsibility for your feelings.

3. **Buts:** Whenever you make an apology that starts with, "I'm sorry, but ... " you're essentially negating your apology. It's another way to shift responsibility. "But" is language that mitigates the level of responsibility. "I'm sorry, but I was tired ...," or "I'm sorry, but I didn't know ... ": When you add "but" to your apology, people tune out.

What should be in your apology?

1. **Commitment to take specific action:** If you're sorry, what are you going to do about it? How are you going to repair the harm that was done? How are you going to prevent further and future harm? Share your plan of action (or at least what steps you're going to take to develop a plan of action.) Developing a plan of action can look like hiring advisors or DEI consultants to figure out the best way to proceed so that your solution doesn't make things worse.

2. **Acknowledgement of harm:** If you're sorry, what are you sorry for? Identify the harm that was done so it's clear what you're apologizing for. Otherwise people will wonder if you really understand what you did. It's better to be clear and transparent about what you think you did wrong.

3. **Clarification of position:** If your position has changed over the course of the conflict and you have changed your mind, or seen the nuance in your earlier position on a topic, share that with your audience. If people have misunderstood where you stand, take the time to clarify. Explain where you stand in relation to what people are upset about and let them make their own decision from a place of values-based alignment.

You can make things right with your audience if you approach your apology with intention. Remember to center the people who were harmed by your actions (not yourself!) and to try to see things from your audience's perspective. That empathy and understanding can help you craft a response that will resonate and help you process what happened and be able to avoid making similar mistakes in the future.

Most of all, I want you to remember you're human, everybody makes mistakes. It's what you do next that matters. You can do hard things, and you've got this. This is learning, this is a journey, this is something that's going to happen over time. This is learning how to be human together.

8
COMMON QUESTIONS ABOUT SOCIAL JUSTICE VALUES IN BUSINESS

Often, when people are considering integrating their values into their business, focusing on diversity and inclusion, or using their business as a force for social justice, they have some common questions. Not knowing the answers can hold them back from taking that next step and might be contributing to their anxiety around doing what they feel is right. This chapter addresses these questions and can hopefully be a resource to alleviate associated fears and help business owners move forward.

Do I Really Have to? Won't This Blow Over?

When we see injustices or social issues as news pegs or headlines without a news cycle, there's an impression that people will stop talking about it eventually. This is true; people might stop talking about certain specific events. But when similar events keep happening, and the issues continue to crop up in the media, it's often because of an underlying injustice driving recurring issues.

When we look at high-profile deaths within historically excluded communities, like George Floyd, people might talk less about that specific person over time, but the underlying lack of justice that drives the circumstances or manner of death means that there will be another incident that will come to the forefront later.

When we look at natural disasters and the extent to which they are impacted by climate change, a specific disaster may resolve itself, but the underlying condition of a planet heating up is going to drive other issues in the future. We can ignore something that's happening now, but something else is going to happen later.

History is full of oppression. Groups that have been facing oppressive conditions have faced similar and different means of oppression over the course of years. Specific instances fade from public conversation, but the issues of race, disability, gender, and sexuality related injustices won't be solved in a news cycle. Humans have been in conflict with each other forever and that is something that can't be changed overnight.

In terms of whether you have to address this or not, that's up to you. If taking action is consistent with your values and you don't do so, you might find that's a source of conflict for you. You may find that you have a sense of dissatisfaction if you're not doing what you could do. Only you can decide if you're OK with not doing anything about something unjust or distressing that you see in the world.

You're a leader in your company and you set the vision. That vision doesn't exist in a vacuum. It's something that is implemented in a world that is in conflict. Your business is likely based on values, even if it's just the prioritization of generating revenue — that's a value. If you are an impact-driven company, it makes sense to talk about what's happening in the world you're trying to impact.

When you think about it, it makes sense even if you aren't an impact-driven company. If something is happening in the world that is impacting your customer base, an expression of empathy to let people know you care about what happens to them isn't a bad thing. That's part of being in a relationship with your audience, them knowing that there is belonging and significance that comes from being part of your community and you value them.

You could also think about it another way: Why are you concerned that people know what you care about, or that you care about what happens to people? Where is the downside to that for you? Is it fear of financial repercussions? Is it fear of backlash and public opinion? Is it your business philosophy to not be personal? Really unpack what's behind the "do I have to?" and look at what's keeping you from feeling like "I get to."

The reality is that building a business is hard work and takes bravery. It takes a lot of courage to step out into the world, assign a value to your ideas, to call people into community, and to be visible.

Brené Brown says, "Daring leaders are never silent about hard things." If you run a business, you're already a daring leader. So the decision to be silent about hard things is up to you at that point, but you're already qualified.

In summary, systemic oppression isn't something that blows over, it takes a lot of work to dismantle, to shift cultural perspectives, to change institutions, to see a transformation in the world. Whether you need to say anything about it or not is your own personal decision based on your comfort level.

How Do I Avoid Looking Like a Bandwagon Jumper?

When something happens and companies respond, there is cynicism that can crop up in the comments, especially if the company doesn't have a history of speaking to social issues. It's natural to not want to look performative when you have something that's really weighing on your heart to speak on.

The best way to avoid looking like a bandwagon jumper is to not be one. Speak on the things that matter to you. Make meaningful efforts to welcome people who are different from you. Have a plan to keep doing that beyond a singular post. It's easy to set an intention to continue talking about an issue, but if you don't have a plan, it may not happen. Life happens, other things become priorities, and it's easy to lose track.

Be consistent in what you talk about and show people you aren't a bandwagon jumper. If you don't want to be seen to be performative, do something that makes an impact. Instead of just posting about something, donate to the cause, make a petition available in your place of business, and give of your time and resources to further the outcome you would like to see.

Taking action is another level of commitment past a seemingly random post that shares a hot take on something that's happening in the world. If an issue impacts your audience, they are invested in it. When you take action on it, you're moving past being a performative bandwagon jumper and investing also.

It's OK to be new to an issue and express that you are learning and educating yourself on it. If you feel like taking action makes you look like a bandwagon jumper, it's a good idea to unpack that. What part of you speaking out feels like an audience wouldn't believe you mean it? Think about the first time you spoke on an issue you really cared about; did you feel the same way you do now? What's different between now and then?

Being concerned about being perceived as a bandwagon jumper is often about other people's expectations and perceptions of you and what you think they are. Speaking out can be a social risk, because there's an opportunity for conflict. But think about the risks to people who are involved with the issue you're going to speak to and what risks they face? How does the social risk you take in speaking about their risks compare? You might find that you can speak on an issue and be fine, but if nobody speaks for people facing a difficult situation, they may not be OK.

If you saw a burning building and didn't call it in, because other people were probably calling, that's what we call a bystander effect. Feeling like you don't have to do something because other people are, that's something that gets in the way of anybody calling. Don't be afraid to sound the alarm because you think someone else is doing it already. You might save a life.

The thing is, racism and other forms of oppression are deadly. You probably won't die from posting something in support of something happening in the world. However, people impacted by the issue could be permanently negatively impacted by it. Is being afraid of looking foolish reason enough not to intervene in some way?

In short, if you don't want to look like a bandwagon jumper, take meaningful action, unpack what your resistance is about, and consistently talk about what you care about if you really care about it.

I'm Just One Person, Will It Make a Difference?

When you see big companies make sizable donations, invest lots of hours, and implement big initiatives, it can feel intimidating. What can one small business really do? What impact can you have on the world as only one person?

I remember one of my clients talking about seeing a large donation being made by a large company; she felt deflated, like she would never be able to make a donation of that size because her business wasn't big enough. She wished she had the resources to do something like that.

In my interview with Megan Hale, she said, "It's so easy to discredit what we are doing, when we put it in perspective of how much needs to be done. If we were to think about a parallel process of growing a business, or writing a book, for instance, if we only focus on what we get done in a day compared to how far we have to go, then it's going to feel like not much. Our work, through the 'enoughness' lens, is to honor every single step, because every single step matters.

"That incremental improvement is what's key and just acknowledging you have to start somewhere." Hale continued and said, "This is where I see a lot of people get stuck, because when we get overwhelmed, we tend to get paralyzed. What's really important is to just focus on that first little step first, and the next step, and next step, and this is going to be lifelong work.

"It's a practice; it's a way of viewing the world and running your business and living your life and all of those things. But if you stay committed to equitable practices, then it just continues to build and layer on over time."

You might not have the reach of Apple or Amazon. You might have a small audience and a small budget, but you can make a difference. Think about this: You trust your online presence to sell what you have on offer. Why would you think it couldn't similarly sell your perspective? Why could it do one and not the other?

Don't underestimate the value of the ripple effect. Your donation, your investment, and/or your voice could inspire others to join you in supporting a cause. You could help shift public opinion on an issue by lending your credibility to it. You could embolden someone else to speak out; think of all the people they could influence. You might be one person, but that's no reason to hold back.

Think back to when you decided to start your business. You were just one person then too. You thought you could offer something people needed and wanted and you went ahead and did that. You, being one person, took a step and started making your mark on the world. You have experience being an influencer for your own business, and you can do the same with a social issue that's important to you.

As the head of your organization, you influence your team to take on and live out your values as expressed in your business. You set the agenda and the focus in terms of your vision. You shape a culture in your organization with your leadership every day. You can do that online as well.

When you wait until you're big and have a lot of money, you miss out on what's possible even with no budget. You can still make some impact and that impact can grow as you do. Here's the secret: Diverse businesses make more money. Studies have shown this, such as one from Forbes ("A Study Finds That Diverse Companies Produce 19% More Revenue," Forbes.com, June 27, 2018). The more you integrate diversity into your business, the greater impact you can make. This has a snowball effect.

When your messaging reflects that you value people who are different from you, it can make you more attractive as an employer. When you have more diverse people solving problems better, you have more money, people, time, and voices to change the world in some way.

If you don't think a person can make a positive impact, think about a time where you felt discouraged during an interaction, where you worked with someone who left you feeling small, who made you dread coming to work or kept you up at night worried about what happens next. We've likely all experienced bullying or abusive behavior at some point. If one person can make a difference for you negatively, how could you as one person make a positive difference?

When you gather in a group and someone tells a racist joke or anecdote, it only takes one person to say "Hey, that's not OK!" to change the expectation of what constitutes acceptable behavior. Similarly, when you go first, others might feel comfortable challenging those behaviors in the future. Just like Sonya Perkins stood up to a supplier that was overpackaging its products, you can stand up to something, too.

Planting a seed for harvest today will pay off down the road. Seeds are pretty small, but an entire food system is built on them. If we didn't start with seeds, it would be next to impossible to feed people. In the beginning, what you can do might not feel like a lot. But you have to start somewhere and that influence can grow over time, just like a garden.

I have a Team, How Do I Keep Everyone on Message?

It's one thing to share your message with the world when it's only you, but how do you handle things when there is more than one person handling communications for the company and engaging with clients online?

It's important to be clear with your team about what you believe in, what the parameters are, and how that should shape communications. For example, if your position is that your company should comply with local health orders in relation to stopping the spread of COVID-19, you might explain to the team exactly that. "In our business, we follow local health orders to keep customers safe."

You might have personal views around masking or vaccines, but it might be that you establish a company line that says, "We encourage all customers to follow local health guidance around masking to stop the spread. We believe vaccination supports public health measures and keeps our community strong."

Similarly, you might establish what isn't said: "We don't tell customers who are against vaccines that they are stupid or engage in debates," or "If our industry is not required to participate in proof of vaccination measures, we do not comment on them." It's important to let your staff know where you stand, how far you are willing to go, and what is off limits for communications coming from the company accounts.

It might seem basic, but if someone is handling your communications and you haven't been clear, it can be challenging to enforce boundaries and confusing for your staff to know what to do. If they know you feel a certain way personally, they might feel empowered to be your voice on an issue where you might not be open to that being part of your communications.

Do I Need to Be an Expert?

You don't need to be an expert to speak on what's happening around you. You can amplify the voices of experts, your customers, and staff who have been impacted and trusted news sources on an issue. Every day, people are impacted by social injustices and every day, people can speak on that.

Being anti-oppressive is a practice. It takes time to grow, like a muscle. Just like your impact will grow over time, so will your breadth and depth of knowledge. Keep reading, keep researching, keep consulting with people further along in their journey, and keep listening. You don't have to be an expert, but you can keep learning.

If not being an expert is holding you back from speaking out, spend some time thinking about what being an expert looks like to you. Also, think about other topics you discuss without being an expert. What makes you feel qualified to speak on those topics and not this one?

There is a school of thought that if you don't know much about something, you tend to overestimate how much you know about it. If you know a little or a lot, you have a better understanding of how much you don't know about something because you have a deeper sense of the scale of the associated issues and the complexities.

What that means is that you've started on your journey of learning about diversity issues, you're probably more cautious about sharing your expertise than someone who has not started or has only tangential exposure to the concepts. People less qualified than you are likely speaking on a topic with no concern for the impacts. I'm not saying to present yourself as an expert because you've taken some classes and read some articles, but I am saying that it's OK to have an opinion on the topic and to talk about that.

There's also something to be said for lived experiences. If you happen to be a member of a group that has been historically excluded, your experiences navigating the world in that identity is also expertise. You don't need to be certified or have a degree to be able to share your perspective and experiences.

One of the quotes that I've heard is that the journey to being antiracist is about committing to addressing racism wherever you find it, even within yourself. You don't have to wait until you have no bias before you speak on social issues. This comes back to the issue of moral perfectionism.

You don't have to be perfect to talk about anti-oppressive practices in your business. It's not like a video game, there is no "boss" at the end of the anti-oppression level that you have to beat to speak on these topics. You don't need to be recognized or have a certificate to have situational awareness and informed opinions on things that are happening in the world.

Do your homework and explore both your position and its counterarguments so you can confidently speak to the topic at hand. You don't have to be an expert, you just have to inform yourself. Something to keep in mind is that if informing yourself includes consulting with people from historically excluded identities, make sure that you compensate them for their labor and find out what their boundaries are for those conversations. Consider your sources outside (or internal) consultants and make sure to pay them for their expertise. In this instance, you aren't just looking at degrees on the wall but also lived experiences. Talk to them about what they are willing to discuss and not willing to discuss and honor those boundaries.

In times of strife, there is a hypervisibility that members of historically excluded groups are subjected to that means people want to learn more about their experiences and their opinions on things. Social media posts circulate about "check on your Black friend" when there has been violence or death impacting a community, but these contacts — if outside of normal communication patterns— can feel invasive, triggering ,or uncomfortable for the recipients of the contact.

It's kind of like a telescoping effect where you might perceive events to have happened more recently if they are more important or impactful, you might overestimate your proximity to the person in question. It can be traumatic to be there when you have dealt with oppression your whole life and someone is just learning about it and being horrified by it. There's a sense of responsibility to take care of the feelings of the person realizing these truths and that's a big burden to impose on someone actually impacted by the issue.

Ultimately, be mindful of getting consent when consulting people in your circle around traumatic topics, have a healthy respect for expertise but don't feel like you have to wait for your anti-oppression decoder ring to come in the mail before you can say that oppression is wrong. It's enough to be a human seeing something happening that's wrong to say it's wrong. If you have questions, ask around, but pay the people who do labor on your behalf.

Values Are Personal: Why Tell My Customers or Audience What I Think?

It used to be that we could compartmentalize, that our personal values were our business and we had the impression we could leave our personal beliefs at the door and just go to work. Now, with the rise of the personal brand, people are more curious than ever to get to know the people behind their favorite products.

In the same way that Millennials want a narrative form of advertising that has an origin story — they want to know the whole story of where their coffee table was born or what music was playing when you came up with their favorite flavor of artisanal popsicles — people want to know more about what drives and inspires you as the head of the business. This was illustrated in a July 23, 2012 article called "4 actionable insights for marketing to Millennials and Gen Z" by Campaign US (www.campaignlive.com/article/4-actionable-insights-marketing-millennials-gen-z/1723084, accessed November 2021).

Certainly you can take the position that that is nobody's business, and that's your call. But when you do share yourself, you give people the chance to choose you. I talk to my clients about the difference between being a chicken strip or a hot wing. Chicken strips are bland but not polarizing, they tend not to generate a lot of excitement but they are quietly tolerated. Hot wings, on the other hand, have wild, raving fans; people who are in search of the perfect sauce; they have competitions and cult followings. You can choose to be a chicken strip and be benignly tolerated, or you can be a hot wing and have a fan base of people who love your boldness.

People don't want to support the implementation of things that are harmful to people who share their identity or who are members of groups they care about. If your politics support the marginalization of people, you might find that people may not want to do business with you. Similarly, there are people who love that and will want to do business with you.

What it comes down to is, as the rallying cry goes, the personal is political. Your personal viewpoint and the causes and initiatives you support impact the daily lives of your customer base. They don't want to spend money with people who make their life harder, no matter which identity they fall under. This is true of people who have been historically excluded and also of people who feel like this is all a bit much and the status quo should be maintained.

Ultimately, when you think you are staying neutral by not making a statement, you are placing a vote for the status quo. It might be that that is in alignment with your values, but if it's not, your silence is not helping your cause. If you want to make waves, you need to actually get in the water.

People want to know where their leader stands because they also want to bring their whole selves to work. This is where employees feel challenged in "apolitical" workplaces. When a person from a normative identity group talks about their experiences, that's a slice of life. When someone from a historically excluded group talks about their experiences, that's often deemed "political."

When only certain people get to talk about their lives outside of work because it's not considered political, there's an erosion to that sense of belonging and significance, there's disengagement, and disillusionment. There's a breakdown in the team because some people are "more equal" than others. It can be a problem for retention and when word gets around, it can be a problem for recruitment.

If you want to be known as a workplace where these politics are off-limits, your hiring pool is going to be more representative of people who can't afford to have a value around where they work, or people who don't care about the experiences of historically excluded people. You reduce the opportunities your staff have to practice empathy.

What happens to the quality of your client service when you have a bunch of people with an empathy gap? Is that something you really want to find out? Probably not. Do you want to see what kind of marketing gets created in an environment where empathy is discouraged? The most effective marketing is empathetic in its creation because you have to intimately understand the before-and-after state in order to sell. You need to be empathetic about what audience members are interested in to curate or create content.

Creating an empathy vacuum doesn't serve your business in the long term. As a leader, you can be a voice around the importance of empathy, about recognizing the challenges of historically excluded populations, and of the need to develop solutions to integrate your values into your business and your corporate culture.

Your values are personal, but you are the leader and you can be a person with your employees, your customers, and your suppliers and the world won't end. The world won't end because people find out you care about people. The world won't end because you show up as yourself. When you show up as yourself, you give others permission to do the same. When your staff show up as themselves, everybody wins.

Megan Hale offered this encouragement. "I think the fear is that if we are too bold and clear with where we stand, now we're going to lose profit, we're going to lose money, we're going to lose people. I have not found that to be true at all; my business has only grown because of what I stand for. People who see that these are my values, they want to spend money with me, they want to support my business, they want to be part of my communities, because we have an alignment there. Has that repelled some people? Absolutely, absolutely. And I want it to because my job is to help people make more money. I want to help businesses who share common values make more money, because I know where that money is going to go and I know the impact that it's going to have. So, of course, I want to be very clear about that from the start."

Who Can Help Me Implement These Strategies?

One of the easiest answers as to who can help implement all your new plans is a diversity, equity, and inclusion (DEI) consultant, an antiracism coach, or an inclusive marketing expert. Look for professionals already working in the field who have an established track record in the area about which you are concerned. If you can't afford to hire someone full or part time to work on diversity issues, you can explore hourly consultations, a contracted, fractional Chief Diversity Officer role, or a workshop facilitator who can guide you through a select topic.

There are companies that can provide focus testing of your inclusive marketing ideas so you can have a heads up if you are contemplating something likely to backfire. You can hire sensitivity readers to review your content and speak to anything problematic that needs addressing. You can establish your own (paid!) board to review ideas and discuss things through a diversity lens. There are so many ways to collaborate on this topic.

There is a temptation, when you have hired a diverse team of staff members, to draw on those people to give you their diversity-related opinions. If that's your intention, it's important to consider how to compensate them for those efforts.

If they are doing the same job as members of the team who have not been historically excluded, and they have more to do at work because they both do the job and the ad hoc diversity consulting, that can feel extractive, exploitative, and unfair. It could be a barrier to retention.

When you are deciding on seeking the opinions of people from historically excluded groups, keep in mind that identities are not monolithic. One Black person doesn't speak for all Black people. There are many Indigenous traditions, perspectives, and cultural norms which vary vastly based on geography, religious practices, personal experiences, and other factors. Don't be the person who excuses mistakes because they "have a Black friend." You may be overestimating their willingness to educate or correct you, even if they are really OK with what is going on; just because your one Black friend is OK with it, doesn't mean anyone who has a problem with it is wrong.

Beyond the fact that everyone has different comfort levels and attitudes toward discrimination, the reality is that oppressive attitudes around racism, ableism, and sexism are in our environment and it's not just people with normative identities who are impacted. People belonging to those groups who have experienced oppression based on their identities may be carrying around internalized racism, ableism, misogyny, transphobia, or other forms of oppression that has weaved itself into their own narrative about themselves and others.

This is why diversity work isn't just a white-people problem, or an able-bodied-people problem, or a straight-person problem. We all have unconscious biases that can get in the way of the way we relate to each other or evaluate whether something is problematic. The difference is that when someone who isn't a member of those groups has those attitudes, there's a power structure attached and it can be even more damaging. This is partly why "reverse racism" doesn't really exist.

Other resources to help you on your journey towards inclusion are articles, books like this, podcasts, group coaching programs, continuing education in the workplace, and online membership communities geared towards social justice. Self-directed and self-initiated learning can be so helpful in creating a foundation of awareness that can help you on your way. We have included a resource list in the downloadable forms kit included with this book (see back of the book for URL).

When you're hiring, vet your sources in the same way that you would a news source. Do your homework on the quality of thought leadership someone has, whether they are respected in their field, how they are seen by their peers, and what has been written about them. Be aware of the possibility of bias by people of historically included people when evaluating the work and expertise of historically excluded people.

Sometimes the mental map of what an expert can look like needs to be updated. For so long, "experts" looked like old white men with university degrees who were on TV. Challenge your own assumptions on what makes someone qualified and be open to receiving feedback and advice from someone whose life experiences vary greatly from your own.

Ultimately, there are people who do this work as their entire job you can hire, there are resources at a wide range of price points from free to a considerable investment but whoever you decide to engage to support you on your journey, make sure they are compensated for their labor equitably so that your learning doesn't become their unpaid responsibility.

9

WHAT'S IN A NAME? A PROFILE OF A COMPANY DOING RIGHT BY FIXING A PROBLEM (ONE LAX)

One Lax is a lacrosse equipment company that found itself embroiled in controversy over its name.

Back in Chapter 4, we talked about how the word "savage" has been a racial slur against Indigenous people. One Lax's old name integrated what was seen to be an abbreviation of the slur, and given the Indigenous origins of the game of lacrosse, this was something that stirred some backlash.

On September 28, One Lax addressed the controversy in a tweet:

> Our company was built on the skill, determination, and competitive spirit required to excel in lacrosse. One year ago, we rebranded to reinforce this connection and better represent the greater lacrosse community, attempting to remove anything that could be offensive to the community we have embraced with our work. We now know we did not go far enough.

After much personal reflection, important discussion and honest conversations with key stakeholders, we apologize to the Indigenous community and the general public for operating under a name that caused hurt, pain and discomfort. We did not do enough to clarify our name in relation to the negative connotations for Indigenous peoples. We will be rebranding immediately to further evolve our brand, becoming a company everyone is proud to see on the field and the floor. Our new name will be a celebration of lacrosse and representative of unity, collaboration, and inclusion.

We believe in the collective impact of our diverse communities and will be taking action by donating to support Indigenous athletes in the pursuit of this incredible sport. Details will be shared in the coming days.

What I appreciate about the way this was handled was that the impact was not minimized, the audience was not blamed for their reactions or concerns, and there was clarity around where the communication breakdown took place. There was clear ownership over the issue, there was an explanation as to the intent of the choice, and there was a roadmap laid out for repair.

The tweet was descriptive of the process the company was already going through to address the issue, and a commitment to further communication. Reparations were promised and an intention was set as to the spirit and values that would be reflected through the actions that would follow.

Essentially, it said, "This is what we were trying to do, it wasn't enough, we are going to do more, this is what we believe as a company, this is our plan, this is how we are giving back, and we are going to keep talking about this."

When you get into a situation as a business owner where you're facing backlash or concerns, do not sweep things under the rug or hide from the discomfort. A commitment to ongoing conversations is a way to bravely and openly face issues and provide the transparency your audience needs to reestablish trust and connection.

On October 5, One Lax announced its rebrand and new name in a tweet:

Let us reintroduce ourselves: We are One Lax, a lacrosse equipment company committed to innovation, expertise and competition. Partnering with athletes to empower the lacrosse community, One lax aims to inspire those who love the game to achieve new levels of performance.

We experience the power of teamwork and collaboration on the field and the floor. One Lax is a celebration of the Creator's Game and represents unity, collaboration and inclusion. We come together to play this incredible sport and we look forward to working with athletes on the field and on the floor.

We are also excited to announce we are in conversations with several highly reputable organizations involved with Indigenous athletes, working with the right organizations to have the best impact is important to us. Thank you for your patience as we determine how One Lax will be an active, supportive partner in the development of Indigenous athletes and improving competition at the highest levels of lacrosse with their talent. We hope to announce this partnership soon.

One Sport. One Community. One Lax.

The rebrand announcement integrated a name that had removed the word about which the audience had concerns. Given the divisive nature of language with negative connotations based on race, the vision of unity put forth through the name was an embodiment of the values shared in their original message. It used "Lax," which the lacrosse community uses as a shortened version of "lacrosse."

The message was positive, pointed to organizational values, highlighted a focus on inclusion, included an acknowledgment of the origin of the sport, and provided more information on ongoing action. I see the "One Sport. One Community. One Lax." tagline to be a call to action to inspire the community to join the journey forward.

The challenge that happens when a brand skips to the unity without doing the acknowledgment of harm, action plan, implementation of corrections, and reparations is that the issues at hand don't get dealt with, people don't feel heard and the impression is given that unity is more important than justice. One Lax didn't skip the work before using language to bring their audience together. I have a lot of respect for that.

I spent some time talking to the One Lax team about what that experience was like. Cofounder Scott Fitchett said the experience was "an enlightening one and an educational one. As passionate humans, people that believe in equality, and people that love lacrosse, based on how everything unfolded with the audience and the perception of the name, we decided that it was best to reposition ourselves, and use the misunderstanding as an opportunity to take our platform and set a benchmark for change and for openness.

"It hurt personally for a while because that's not who we were," Fitchett acknowledged, but he and his business partners are focused on the future and the opportunity that they are able to seize to connect more with their audience and their industry partners moving forward.

"It's something that we're really going to take and run with and it's going to really shape the future of our business and hopefully the future of the game with creating more collaboration and involving conversations like we're having right now with savvy interested people ... who want to hear our story and want to tell the story so that maybe the world's a better place tomorrow," he elaborated.

"It's not something that we meant to do, so it was important for us to be able to come out and tell people who we were and tell our story and apologize without any ill intent, and really rectify everything. Part of our story is being open and creating collaboration and valuing cultures," he continued.

Fitchett pointed to the diversity of their hometown of Scarborough and how their business aims to embody the value of inclusion that reflects their community. The rebrand came at a cost, and resulted in some waste in merchandise at a time where supply chain challenges have been an issue, but ultimately they feel the change is for the better and is consistent with their responsibility as business owners.

Fitchett spoke to that, explaining, "I think there's a large responsibility on business owners and especially big corporate business owners and investors and shareholders to really take a look at what's happened in the last couple of years with the pandemics and what's happened in the last 100 years with oppression and genocide, and all these awful things that have happened, and really use the future as an opportunity to lift each other up. I don't know if that's necessarily business advice but I think that's just human advice because the more we work toward profits and away from each other and away from our neighbors and try and make our house bigger than our neighbor's house, and our food better than our neighbor's food, the worse off everyone becomes."

One Lax had an unintended image problem with their brand that gave the wrong impression about who it was, and it took on the problem head on, in a relationship-focused way, and prioritized communication. Its focus on the triple bottom line, the situational awareness of what its audience is dealing with on a day-to-day basis, the empathy, and the corporate social responsibility is consistent with the spirit of *Stay Woke, Not Broke* and why their story was selected to close this book.

This is a story of redemption, connection, bravery, and an example of the way you can come back from a challenge and build something even better, build deeper relationships, and reposition yourself in the market. Obviously as business owners you want to avoid harm, and want to have positive relationships but the reality is that when things happen, there is a path forward if you are transparent, brave, and motivated enough to take those important steps toward a brighter future in your business.

You don't have to be perfect. You just have to be willing to commit to the process, take action, and keep doing the next right thing.

CONCLUSION:
A CALL TO ACTION

Being woke doesn't have to mean being broke. You can have a mission-driven organization that has a healthy triple bottom line. You can make money and keep growing. You can hire more people, make a bigger impact in your community, and contribute more to being the change in the world that you want to see.

I undertook diversity work because it's reflective of my values and I want people to have the experience that I have: Bringing my whole self to everything that I do. I have experience helping people in the public sector, the private sector, and the nonprofit/charitable sector integrate values into the way they do business and learn how to talk about it.

Ultimately, diversity and inclusion have to be more than words to be effective. That's why it's important to look at what diversity and inclusion means in your business, how your language and policies can be updated to include more people, how your marketing can reflect your values, and how you can build an online community of which you can be proud.

When you first picked up this book you might have been asking yourself a variety of questions around whether you can or even should implement strategies surrounding social justice.

I hope these questions have been answered and that you've been able to learn from the examples and experiences I shared in this book.

Where Do I Go from Here?

What should you do now?

- **Talk it out:** Take what you've learned and talk to your team. Talk to the people with whom you normally discuss business changes. Talk to your partner, your family, your neighbor and your friends. Talk to the people who matter to you and talk about the issues you consider important. Get practice talking about those things so it feels more natural when you're doing it in your business.

- **Listen and learn:** Take the time to educate yourself. Ask questions in your peer group. Invest in the knowledge of diversity and inclusion experts. Listen to podcasts, read articles, read books like this one and others from people who have different experiences and identities. Don't stop learning.

- **Be brave:** If making a public statement where you tell people you care about what happens to them is a major point of concern or contention, be glad you are not in a position where you face the challenges of the people you claim to care about. Talking about social issues is scary. The consequences of not doing so are deadly. Be brave.

- **Make time:** Create a plan for your learning and dedicate time to your studies. Without a clear plan, learning about diversity goes on the never-ending to-do list and you won't get around to it. I often hear people say "But I don't have time to learn about racism" and let me tell you, as an Indigenous business owner, I don't have time to experience it. But racism doesn't care if you have time for it. It doesn't care if I have time for it. It is going to keep happening if we don't keep taking the time to dismantle oppressive cultures.

- **Release the overwhelm:** When you think about dismantling power structures, decolonizing, or smashing the patriarchy, it can all sound very overwhelming. That might seem like too big of a goal or a goal you're not qualified to undertake. Break your actions into steps and create a plan to address them. Rome wasn't built in a day.

- **Pace yourself:** One of the things I find most often when clients start on their journey, they feel pressured to jump into every fight. They are exhausted trying to learn all the things, to make a statement on everything, and feel like they are letting people down if they aren't everywhere. Nobody wants a burnt out ally. You aren't useful that way. What you post online is just one part of the way you make a difference. The way you interact with your people, give funds, volunteer, protest, or any number of other things count, too.

- **Dial in on what matters to you:** It's OK to focus your efforts. Nobody says, "That David Suzuki ... what's he done about diabetes research lately?" People who know of him know he focuses on the environment. You can have an area of focus and refer people to others who are speaking on other issues that you know less about or are less connected to. You don't have to have an opinion on everything.

- **Bring your own humility:** It's OK to say you don't know something. You don't have to have all the answers. You can tell people you're going to go away and study and consult (but actually do it). Urgency is sometimes considered a tool of white supremacy. It undermines the need to rest. It applies pressure that everything has to be now, instant, and on demand. You don't have to operate that way. You can take your time.

- **Take stock:** Go through the Is Your Business Ready to Welcome Everyone? checklist and see where you land.

- **Give Yourself Grace.** It can be uncomfortable learning and it can be hard to change your perspective on things over time. There might be deeply rooted reasons why you believe things. You've been impacted by experiences in the past that have shaped who you are. Change is hard and it's OK to acknowledge that. The way you do that and where you do that and who you do that with is important though.

- **Be situationally aware:** Talking about how hard it is to learn how to respect people who have been historically excluded with someone from that demographic can be awkward (unless that is the context of your relationship, they are coaching you on these things). This might be a better conversation for your therapist, your journal, or other people who you share an identity with who are also on a learning journey.

- **Give grace (to yourself and others!):** When we make mistakes, we need to treat it as an opportunity to learn how to do it better next time. You can't change the past but you can change the future. You can do all the things that you can do in order to try and make things as inclusive as possible but there still might be something you miss because you're human, because things change over time, standards change, technology changes, and there's also human error. All of these things that can get in the way so give yourself grace and move on after making your best efforts at repair.

Integrating diversity, equity, inclusion, and social justice is an achievable goal for a business of any size. You don't have to wait to be big enough, to have enough money, to know enough. You can get started today. You don't have to have all of the answers, but you do have to be willing to look for them and to ask for them. As long as you're willing to listen to people who have been historically excluded, from different walks of life, who have different experiences, that's what you need to be successful.

You can stay woke, not broke, and you can build your triple bottom line. You can do the right thing and make money at the same time. You can build an inclusive community around your brand and you can lead people towards the social change you want to see in the world. The world right now is full of chaos, but I love the expression, "When nothing is certain, anything is possible." What will you do to create possibilities? I can't wait to find out.

Best of luck to you,

Alison
Twitter: @alliespins

Checklist
Is Your Business Ready to Welcome Everyone?

Your Position

[ ] Do you have a diversity statement?

[ ] Did you write it yourself or was it written for you specifically?

[ ] Can you explain it in your own words if someone asks about it?

[ ] Does your statement explain how social justice values are integrated into your brand experience?

Gender Issues

[ ] If you are open to working with people of all genders, is that clear from your copy?

[ ] If you have made specific changes to make your business accessible and welcoming to people of all genders is that included in your copy?

[ ] Is your marketing free of gender stereotyping and content that reinforces gender as a binary?

Disability Issues

[ ] Is your website accessible?

[ ] Do you use alt text to describe images?

[ ] Is your design screen reader friendly?

[ ] Do you have alt text on images that feature embedded text that a screen reader can't read?

[ ] Do you have transcripts or captions for audio or video format?

[ ] Is your font dyslexia friendly?

Race Issues

[ ] Do your images reflect the true diversity of your client base?

[ ] Is your content free of gifs or memes that feature people of a color that don't reflect you? (This is digital blackface.)

[ ] Have you avoided using African American Vernacular English/Black Vernacular English in your copy (language that sounds Black) stylistically to be trendy? (This can be problematic.)

[ ] Do you have a land or territory acknowledgement on your website?

Intersectional Issues

[ ] Are your payment plans equitable and consistent with your values?

[ ] Does your content reflect the role of your products and services in the context of experiences of lives of people who aren't like you?

[ ] Do you give back to any of the social issues you say that you care about?

[ ] Is it easy for people to find where your give-back funds go?